1 / Parts of Speech

Words—the building blocks of sentences—can be divided into eight parts of speech. **Parts of speech** are classifications of words according to their meaning and use in a sentence.

This section will explain the eight parts of speech:

nouns	prepositions	conjunctions
pronouns	adjectives	interjections
verbs	adverbs	

1a   Nouns

A **noun** is a word that is used to name something: a person, a place, a thing, or an idea.

Nouns are classified in various ways:

Proper nouns and common nouns. A **proper noun** refers to someone or something specific and is capitalized (*Alice Walker, Chicago, July*). All other nouns are **common nouns** (*woman, city, month*). (See 23g, page 36.)

Singular and plural nouns. A **singular noun** names one person, place, thing, or idea (*boy, alley, truth*). A **plural noun** refers to two or more persons, places, things, or ideas. Most singular nouns can be made plural with the addition of an *s* (*boys, alleys, truths*). Some nouns, like *box*, have irregular plurals (*boxes*). You can check on nouns you think may have irregular plurals by looking up the singular form in a dictionary. (See 2a, page 4.)

Collective nouns. A collective noun refers to a group of persons or things that is generally thought of as one unit. Examples are *group, jury*, and *team*. (See 6d, page 12.)

Count and noncount nouns. **Count nouns** name persons, places, things, or ideas that can be counted (*one man, two cities, three balls, four questions*). **Noncount nouns** name things that come in forms that cannot be counted (*flour, air, affection*). (See "Articles with Count and Noncount Nouns," page 48.)

1b   Pronouns

A **pronoun** is a word that stands for a noun. Pronouns eliminate the need for constant repetition. Compare the following two examples:

Lisa met Lisa's friends in the record store at the mall. Lisa meets Lisa's friends there every Saturday.

Lisa met **her** friends in the record store at the mall. **She** meets **them** there every Saturday.

> The pronoun *her* is used to replace the word *Lisa's*. The pronoun *she* replaces *Lisa*. The pronoun *them* replaces the words *Lisa's friends*.

Personal pronouns. A personal pronoun refers to a particular person, place, or thing. It can act in a sentence as subject, object, or possessive.

Singular: I, me, my, mine, you, your, yours, he, him, his, she, her, hers, it, its

Plural: we, us, our, ours, you, your, yours, they, them, their, theirs

Relative pronouns. A relative pronoun refers to a person or thing already mentioned in the sentence. It begins a dependent clause: Here is a watch **that** I found.

who	whose	whom	which	that

Interrogative pronouns. An interrogative pronoun introduces a question: **What** day is this?

who	whose	whom	which	what

Demonstrative pronouns. A demonstrative pronoun is used to point out a particular person or thing: **This** is my car.

this	that	these	those

Do not use *them* (as in *them shoes*), *this here, that there, these here*, or *those there* to point out.

Reflexive pronouns. A reflexive pronoun is one that ends in *-self* or *-selves*. It is used as the object of a verb: Cary cut **herself**. It can also be used as the object of a preposition when the subject of the verb is the same as that object: James sent a birthday card to **himself**.

Singular: myself, yourself, himself, herself, itself
Plural: ourselves, yourselves, themselves

Intensive pronouns. Intensive pronouns have exactly the same forms as reflexive pronouns. The difference is in how they are used. An intensive pronoun is used to add emphasis: I **myself** will need to read the contract before I sign it.

Indefinite pronouns. An indefinite pronoun refers to a nonspecific person or thing.

each	either	everyone	nothing	both
several	all	any	most	none

Reciprocal pronouns. A reciprocal pronoun expresses shared actions or feelings. It refers to individual parts of a plural antecedent: The students help **each other** prepare for finals.

each other	one another

(For more information on pronouns, see 6d, pages 12–13, and "Pronouns," pages 13–16.)

1c   Verbs

Verbs generally express action or being. Every complete sentence must contain at least one verb. There are several categories of verbs.

Action and linking verbs. A verb that expresses action is called an **action verb**. It tells what is happening in a sentence.

Mr. Jensen **swatted** at the bee with his hand.

A verb that expresses a state of being is a **linking verb**. A linking verb joins (or links) the subject of a sentence to a **subject complement**, a word that modifies or renames the subject. Linking verbs are usually forms of *be*.

Forms of the Linking Verb *Be*

am	are	were	have been	had been
is	was	will be	has been	will have been

The sun **is** a star.

> *Is* joins the subject, *sun*, to a word that renames, or identifies, it: *star*.

Verbs such as *look*, *seem*, and *taste* are also linking verbs when they are followed by a subject complement. (For more about subject complements, see 2b, page 5.)

This cucumber **tastes** bitter.

> *Tastes* links the subject, *cucumber*, to a word that modifies it: *bitter*.

Other Common Linking Verbs

look	sound	smell	taste
feel	become	appear	seem

Main and helping verbs. A verb is made up of at least one word, the main verb, plus one or more helping verbs that may precede it.

The basketball team **will be leaving** for a game at six o'clock.

> In this sentence, the main verb is *leaving*. The helping verbs are *will* and *be*. *Leaving* by itself would not make sense as a verb. It would be incorrect to say, "The basketball team leaving for a game at six o'clock." Words that end in *-ing* cannot be the verb of a sentence unless they are accompanied by at least one helping verb.

Oscar **should have worn** a jacket to his job interview.

> In this sentence, *Oscar* is the subject. What should Oscar have done? He *should have worn* (a jacket). *Should* and *have* are helping verbs. The last verb in the phrase, *worn*, is the main verb. *Worn* by itself could not be the verb. It would not be correct to say, "Oscar worn a jacket to his job interview."

The Helping Verbs

Forms of be:	be, am, is, are, was, were, being, been
Forms of have:	have, has, had
Forms of do:	do, does, did
Modals:	can, could, may, might, must, ought (to), shall, should, will, would

Each of the helping verbs can be used alone or in a variety of combinations, such as *have been*, *may be*, *might have been*, and *would have been*.

Modals, unlike other helping verbs, do not change form to indicate tense. In other words, they do not take such endings as *-ed*, *-s*, and *-ing*. After the modals, always use the basic form of a verb, the form in which a verb is listed in the dictionary (*go*, *see*, *work*, and so on).

The factory **will close** tomorrow.

We **should attend** the wedding.

Helping verbs are sometimes called **auxiliary verbs**. (For more about helping verbs, see "Verbs," pages 7–13.)

Transitive and intransitive verbs. A **transitive verb** requires a direct object to complete its meaning. A **direct object** is a word or words that receive the action of the verb and answer such questions as *whom?* or *what?*

The florist **uses** wildflowers.

> *Uses* is a transitive verb. The direct object is *wildflowers*; it answers the question *uses what?*

An **intransitive verb** does not need a direct object to complete its meaning.

Oil **floats**.

Many verbs can be transitive or intransitive depending on their use. For instance, in the following sentence, *floats* is transitive:

My brother **floats** paper boats in the tub.

> In this sentence, *floats* has a direct object—*paper boats*. *Paper boats* answers the question *floats what?*

Phrasal verbs. A phrasal verb is made up of a main verb followed by a particle. A **particle** is a preposition that functions as part of the verb. The particle gives the verb a different meaning than it has by itself. For example, the particle *up* changes the verb *look* to *look up*: **Look up** the definition in the dictionary. There are numerous phrasal verbs, including *call up*, *find out*, *hand in*, *make up*, and *put off*.

When your papers are done, **hand** them **in**.

Let's hug and **make up**.

Words that are not verbs. Here are some tips to help you find the verb in a sentence:

- The verb of a sentence never begins with the word *to*.

  > The instructor agreed to provide ten minutes for study before the quiz.

  > Although *provide* is a verb, *to provide* cannot be the verb of a sentence. The verb of this sentence is *agreed*.

  (For more information on verbs that follow the word *to*, see 3b, page 5, and 13b, page 23.)

- Certain adverbs—such as *not*, *just*, *never*, *only*, and *always*—may appear between the main verb and the helping verb. They describe the verb, but they are never part of it.

  > The canary **does** not **sing** in front of visitors.

  > We **will** never **eat** at that restaurant again.

1d   Prepositions

A **preposition** is a word that connects a noun or a pronoun to another word in the sentence.

A man **in** the bus was snoring loudly.

> *In* is a preposition. It connects the noun *bus* to *man*.

On the next page is a list of common prepositions.

Common Prepositions

about	before	down	into	through
above	behind	during	like	to
across	below	except	of	toward
after	beneath	for	off	under
among	beside	from	on	up
around	between	in	over	with
at	by	instead of	since	without

A **prepositional phrase** is a group of words that begins with a preposition and ends with a noun or pronoun. The words *in the bus*, for example, are a prepositional phrase. There is a prepositional phrase in the following sentence:

The man **with the black mustache** left the restaurant quickly.

> The noun *mustache* is the object of the preposition *with*. The prepositional phrase *with the black moustache* describes the word *man*. It tells us exactly which man left the restaurant quickly.

(For more about prepositions, see 3a, page 5, and 6d, pages 11–12.)

1e   Adjectives

An **adjective** is a word that describes a noun (the name of a person, place, thing, or idea). Look at the following sentence:

The dog lay down on a mat in front of the fireplace.

Now look at this sentence when adjectives have been inserted:

The **shaggy** dog lay down on a **worn** mat in front of the fireplace.

> The adjective *shaggy* describes the noun *dog*; the adjective *worn* describes the noun *mat*.

Adjectives add spice to our writing. They also help us to identify particular people, places, or things. They can be found in two places:

- An adjective may come before the word it describes: a **damp** night, the **moldy** bread, a **striped** umbrella.

- An adjective that describes the subject of a sentence may come after a linking verb. The linking verb may be a form of the verb *be*: He *is* **furious**. I *am* **exhausted**. They *are* **hungry**. Other linking verbs include *feel, look, sound, smell, taste, appear, seem,* and *become*: The soup *tastes* **salty**. Your hands *feel* **dry**. The dog *seems* **lost**.

The words *a, an,* and *the* (called **articles**) are generally classified as adjectives.

(For more information on adjectives, see "Adjectives and Adverbs," pages 16–17. Also see page 41 for when to use *a* and *an*.)

1f   Adverbs

An **adverb** is a word that describes a verb, an adjective, or another adverb. Many adverbs end in the letters *ly*. Look at the following sentence:

The canary sang in the pet store window as the shoppers greeted each other.

Now look at this sentence after adverbs have been inserted:

The canary sang **softly** in the pet store window as the shoppers **loudly** greeted each other.

The adverbs add details to the sentence. They also allow the reader to contrast the singing of the canary to the noise the shoppers are making.

Look at the following sentences and the explanations of how adverbs are used in each case:

The chef yelled **angrily** at the young waiter.

> The adverb *angrily* describes the verb *yelled*.

My mother has an **extremely** busy schedule on Tuesdays.

> The adverb *extremely* describes the adjective *busy*.

The sick man spoke **very** faintly to his loyal nurse.

> The adverb *very* describes the adverb *faintly*.

Some adverbs do not end in *-ly*. Examples include *very, often, never, always,* and *well*.

(For more information on adverbs, see 2b, pages 4–5, and "Adjectives and Adverbs," pages 16–17.)

1g   Conjunctions

Conjunctions are words that connect. There are three kinds of conjunctions.

Coordinating conjunctions. A coordinating conjunction joins ideas with equal roles in a sentence.

Max and Roger interviewed for the job, but their friend Anne got it.

> The coordinating conjunction *and* connects two proper nouns that are both subjects of the same verb: *Max* and *Roger*. The coordinating conjunction *but* connects two equal word groups (independent clauses): *Max and Roger interviewed for the job* and *their friend Anne got it*.

The Coordinating Conjunctions

and	so	nor	yet
but	or	for	

(For more on coordinating conjunctions, see 5b, page 7; 10c, page 19; and 13a, page 21.)

Correlative conjunctions. Correlative conjunctions, which function in pairs, also join ideas with equal roles in a sentence.

We will **either** repaint the room **or** wallpaper it.

> *Either* and *or* join the two verbs of the sentence: *repaint* and *wallpaper*.

Common Correlative Conjunctions

both . . . and	neither . . . nor	whether . . . or
either . . . or	not only . . . but also	

(For more on correlative conjunctions, see 12a, pages 20–21.)

Subordinating conjunctions. When a subordinating conjunction is added to a clause, the clause can no longer stand alone as an independent sentence. It is no longer a complete thought. For example, look at the following sentence:

Karen fainted in class.

The word group *Karen fainted in class* is a complete thought. It can stand alone as a sentence. See what happens when a subordinating conjunction is added to a complete thought:

When Karen fainted in class.

Now the words cannot stand alone as a sentence. They are dependent on other words to complete the thought:

When Karen fainted in class, we put her feet up on some books.

Common Subordinating Conjunctions

after	because	if	unless	where
although	before	since	until	wherever
as	even if	so that	when	whether
as if	even though	though	whenever	while

(For more information on subordinating conjunctions, see 5b, page 7; 9a, page 18; and 13a, page 22.)

1h Interjections

Interjections are words that are used to express emotion. They have no grammatical connection with the rest of a sentence and can stand alone. Mild interjections are followed by commas; strong ones are followed by exclamation marks. Examples are *oh, wow, ouch,* and *oops.* These words are usually not found in formal writing.

Oh, we're late for class.

"**Hey**!" yelled Maggie. "That's my bike."

1i A note on words being more than one part of speech

A word may function as more than one part of speech. For example, the word *dust* can be a verb or a noun, depending on its role in a sentence.

I **dust** my bedroom once a month, whether it needs it or not. *(verb)*

The top of my refrigerator is covered with an inch of **dust**. *(noun)*

2 / Sentence Basics

A sentence is made up of two basic parts:

1 A **complete subject**—the simple subject and its modifiers;
2 A **predicate**—a verb and its modifiers, objects, and complements.

2a Subjects and their modifiers

The **simple subject** of a sentence is the noun or pronoun—the person, place, thing, or idea—that the sentence is about. The subject usually performs an action or is described by the sentence. The subject can be called the "who or what" word. To find the subject, ask yourself, "Who or what is doing something in this sentence?" or "Who or what is being described in this sentence?"

The players ran onto the field.

Who is doing something in the sentence? The answer is *players*. That's who ran onto the field. So *players* is the subject of the sentence.

The popcorn is overly greasy.

What is being described in this sentence? The answer is *popcorn*. That's what is overly greasy. So *popcorn* is the subject of the sentence.

Singular, plural, and compound subjects. A subject is singular or plural. Most plural subjects simply end in *s*.

Singular: The **car** in front of us is speeding.
Plural:　The **cars** in front of us are speeding.

Some plural subjects are irregular:

Singular: The **child** was crying.
Plural:　The **children** were crying.

(For more information on making nouns plural, see 27e, page 40.)

A **compound subject** is two or more subjects connected by a coordinating conjunction such as *and*. Compound subjects are usually plural. (See 6d, page 12.)

Compound: The **car** and the **truck** in front of us are speeding.

Modifiers. The subject of a sentence may be accompanied by words, phrases, and clauses that modify it.

A very large truck stalled on the bridge.

The subject, *truck*, is modified by the words *a very large*.

Several bunches of green grapes fell onto the supermarket floor.

The subject, *bunches*, is modified by the word *several* and the prepositional phrase *of green grapes*.

The wallet that I lost was never found.

The subject, *wallet*, is modified by the word *the* and the clause *that I lost*.

2b Verbs and their modifiers, complements, and objects

The **verb** of a sentence is the word or words—the main verb and any helping verbs—that express action or being. (See 1c, pages 1–2, for a more complete explanation of verbs.)

The verb and its modifiers. The verb of a sentence may be accompanied by words, phrases, and clauses that modify it.

Traffic **moved slowly**.

The verb *moved* is modified by the adverb *slowly*.

The boy **was waving at the airplane**.

> The verb *was waving* is modified by the prepositional phrase *at the airplane*.

I **sneezed when the instructor called on me**.

> The verb *sneezed* is modified by the clause *when the instructor called on me*.

Compound verbs. A sentence may contain a compound verb—two or more verbs that have the same subject or subjects.

The impatient customer **tapped** her fingers on the counter and **cleared** her throat.

> The subject of this sentence, *customer*, did two things: *tapped* (her fingers) and *cleared* (her throat).

Subject complements. A subject complement follows a linking verb (such as *is, was, were, look, appear,* and *seem*) and provides information about the subject. A subject complement is either an adjective or a noun or pronoun. If it is an adjective, it describes the subject.

This potato is **blue**.

> The verb *is* links the subject, *potato*, to an adjective that describes it: *blue*.

Nouns and pronouns are naming words. When a subject complement is a noun or pronoun, it renames the subject, identifying it in some way.

Cara's boyfriend is **a good mechanic**.

> The verb *is* links the subject, *boyfriend*, to a noun that identifies it: (a good) *mechanic*.

Direct and indirect objects. A **direct object** is a noun or pronoun that receives the action of a verb.

Mr. Duncan built a **bookcase**.

> *Bookcase* is the direct object; it is what was built.

Sometimes a direct object is preceded by an indirect object. The **indirect object** is the noun or pronoun that tells *to whom* or *for whom* the action of the verb is done.

Mr. Duncan built **me** a bookcase.

> *Me* is the indirect object. It tells *for whom* the bookcase was built.

To find out if an object is direct or indirect, try mentally inserting the word *to* or *for* before it. If the word is an indirect object, the sentence will make sense.

Mr. Duncan built [for] **me** a bookcase.

Object complements. An object complement follows a direct object and describes or renames it. An object complement is either an adjective or a noun or pronoun.

My boss made me **angry**.

> The direct object is *me*—that's who received the action of the verb, *made*. The object complement is *angry*, an adjective that describes the direct object.

She called the puppy **Minnie**.

> The direct object is *puppy*—that's what was called something. The object complement is *Minnie*, a proper noun that renames the direct object.

Object complements are found with verbs such as *appoint, call, consider, name,* and *make*.

3 / Phrases

A **phrase** is a word group that never functions as a complete sentence. It may lack a subject, a verb, or both. Phrases function as parts of speech—nouns, verbs, adjectives, and adverbs.

3a   Prepositional phrases

A **prepositional phrase** begins with a preposition (a word such as *from, on,* and *to*) and ends with the object of the preposition. It may also include modifiers of the object.

Prepositional phrases function as adjectives or adverbs. (For a list of prepositions, see 1d, page 3.)

The 1995 earthquake **in Kobe, Japan**, killed more than five thousand people **within minutes**.

> The first prepositional phrase functions as an adjective; it modifies the noun *earthquake*. The second prepositional phrase functions as an adverb; it modifies the verb *killed*.

3b   Verbal phrases

A **verbal phrase** is a word group that contains one of the three types of verbals—infinitives, participles, and gerunds.

Infinitive phrases. An infinitive phrase is made up of *to* plus the base form of a verb (for example, *to go* or *to sing*) and any modifiers or objects. It can function as a noun, adjective, or adverb.

To delay is dangerous.

> *To delay* functions as a noun, the subject of the sentence.

I would like a place **to do my woodworking**.

> *To do my woodworking* functions as an adjective modifying the noun *place*.

The old cat is happy **to sleep all day**.

> *To sleep all day* functions as an adverb modifying the adjective *happy*.

Participial phrases. A participial phrase is made up of a present participle (the *-ing* form of a verb) or a past participle (the *-ed* form of a regular verb or the past participle form of an irregular verb) plus accompanying words. A participial phrase always functions as an adjective.

Bobbing in the air, the round white kite resembled a drunken cloud.

> The participial phrase modifies the noun *kite*.

The instructor smiled, **delighted at the class's enthusiasm**.

> The participial phrase modifies the noun *instructor*.

Frozen with fear, Rashid felt his heartbeat accelerate.

> The participial phrase *frozen with fear* describes the proper noun *Rashid*.

Gerund phrases. A gerund phrase—the *-ing* form of a verb plus any modifiers or objects—always functions as a noun. You can distinguish between a participial phrase that contains the *-ing* form of a verb and a gerund phrase because of their different functions—a participial phrase functions only as an adjective.

> **Spanking children** may cause them to become aggressive toward their peers.

> The gerund phrase serves as the subject of the sentence.

3c   Absolute phrases

An **absolute phrase** usually includes a noun or pronoun followed by a participle or participial phrase. Absolute phrases modify an entire clause or sentence.

> **Dental fear being common**, some dentists advertise a gentle approach.

> The noun *fear* is followed by the participial phrase *being common*.

4 / Clauses

A **clause** is a group of words that has a subject and a verb. There are two types of clauses—independent and dependent.

4a   Independent clauses

An **independent clause** is able to stand alone as a sentence.

> The breeze is chilly.

4b   Dependent clauses

A **dependent clause** cannot stand alone as a sentence. It begins with a word that requires it to be connected to an independent clause.

> **Although** the sun is shining brightly.

The word *although* makes this clause dependent—it must be joined to an independent clause:

> **Although** the sun is shining brightly, the breeze is chilly.

There are three types of dependent clauses. They are named according to their function in a sentence.

Adjective clauses. An adjective clause, like an adjective, can modify a noun or a pronoun. It begins with a relative pronoun, such as *who*, or a relative adverb, such as *where*. Words that commonly begin adjective clauses are listed below.

Words That Begin Adjective Clauses

Relative pronouns:	who, whom, whose, which, that
Relative adverbs:	when, where, why

We gave cereal samples to every customer **who came in today**.

> *Who* refers to *customer*, so the adjective clause modifies *customer*.

There is a rumor **that our apartment building is going to be sold**.

> *That* refers to *rumor*, so the adjective clause modifies *rumor*. The word *that* can be omitted from a dependent clause if the sentence remains clear without it: *There is a rumor our apartment building is going to be sold.*

Adjective clauses may be essential to the meaning of the independent clause or nonessential. Nonessential material is set off by commas.

> The Shu family moved to Cherry Hill, **where the schools are considered excellent**.

Adverb clauses. An adverb clause, like an adverb, can modify a verb, an adjective, or an adverb. It begins with a subordinating conjunction, such as *because* or *if*. Adverb clauses generally explain when, where, why, how, under what condition, to what degree, or with what result.

Words That Begin Adverb Clauses

Subordinating conjunctions:				
after	because	if	unless	where
although	before	since	until	wherever
as	even if	so that	when	whether
as if	even though	though	whenever	while

Tina decided to study more **after she saw her mid-semester grades**.

> The adverb clause modifies the verb *decided*, explaining when Tina decided to study more.

If an adverb clause begins a sentence, it is usually followed by a comma.

> **After she saw her mid-semester grades,** Tina decided to study more.

Noun clauses. Noun clauses begin with some of the same words that adjective clauses begin with. Unlike adjective clauses, however, noun clauses do not modify. A noun clause can function in the same ways that a single noun does, including as a subject, a subject complement, and a direct object. A noun clause may begin with a pronoun such as *who* or *whoever* or with a subordinating conjunction such as *when* or *where*. Words that commonly begin noun clauses are listed below.

Words That Begin Noun Clauses

Relative and related pronouns:	who, whoever, whom, whomever, whose, what, whatever, that, which, whichever
Subordinating conjunctions:	when, whenever, where, wherever, how, why, if, whether

What you see is **what you get**.

> The first noun clause is the subject of the sentence; its verb is *is*. The second noun clause is the subject complement.

The plastic spider on the wall tile surprises **whoever enters the shower**.

> The noun clause is the direct object of the verb *surprises*.

5 / Sentence Types

Sentences can be classified according to their purpose or their structure.

5a   The four sentence types based on purpose

Declarative sentences. A declarative sentence makes a statement. Most sentences are declarative.

> The average human body is covered with fourteen to eighteen square feet of skin.

Interrogative sentences. An interrogative sentence asks a question.

> Where are we?

Imperative sentences. An imperative sentence gives a command, makes a request, or offers advice. Generally the subject, *you*, is omitted, but understood.

> Stay away from that closet.

Exclamatory sentences. An exclamatory sentence expresses sudden strong emotion. It is often an incomplete sentence.

> You've come back!
>
> What a game!

5b   The four sentence types based on structure

Sentences can be divided into four types according to how many and what kind of clauses they contain. (See "Clauses," page 6.)

Simple sentences. A simple sentence is made up of a single independent clause. (Below, subjects are *italicized*, and verbs are **boldfaced**.)

> A *jet* **soared** through the darkening sky.
>
> Several *customers* **complained** about the slow service.

A simple sentence may have a compound subject, a compound verb, or both.

> *Shorts* and *T-shirts* **sway** on the clothesline.
>
> The *children* **splashed** and **squealed** in the swimming pool.
>
> Every weekend, *Gary*, *Chet*, and *Rita* **go** to the movies, **eat** at a Chinese restaurant, and **dance** at a club.

Compound sentences. A compound sentence is made up of two or more independent clauses. The two clauses may be joined by a comma and a coordinating conjunction (such as *and*, *but*, or *so*) or by a semicolon.

> Rose wants chili for dinner, **but** she forgot to buy beans.
>
> > This sentence is made up of two independent clauses joined by a comma and the coordinating conjunction *but*.
>
> The plane landed safely; everyone felt relief.
>
> > The two independent clauses are joined by a semicolon.

(For a complete list and explanation of coordinating conjunctions, see 1g, page 3.)

Complex sentences. A complex sentence includes one independent clause and at least one dependent one. When a dependent clause begins a sentence, it is generally followed by a comma. In the following sentence, the dependent clause is boldfaced:

> **Although nearby trees were blown down**, our house escaped the tornado.
>
> > The first clause begins with the subordinating conjunction *although*, so it depends on the independent clause to finish the thought.

Compound-complex sentences. A compound-complex sentence has the characteristics of both a compound sentence and a complex sentence. Like the compound sentence, the compound-complex sentence includes at least two independent clauses. Like the complex sentence, it contains at least one dependent clause. In the following example, the dependent clause is boldfaced:

> **When the children's parents were out of town**, the babysitter had parties, and the children watched TV until midnight.
>
> > The two independent clauses are connected by the coordinating conjunction *and*. Together they could make a compound sentence: *The babysitter had parties, and the children watched TV until midnight.* The dependent clause begins with the subordinating conjunction *when*. Combined with either of the two independent statements, it would make a complex sentence, for example: *When the children's parents were out of town, the babysitter had parties.*

6 / Verbs

6a   Verb tenses

The four principal parts of verbs. Each verb tense is formed with one of the four principal parts of verbs. Following are explanations of each of these verb parts.

1 Basic form. The basic form is the form in which verbs are listed in the dictionary (the infinitive form). It is used for the present tense for all subjects except third-person singular subjects.

> I **ask** questions in class.

Third-person singular verbs are formed by adding -*s* to the basic form.

> Dalila always **asks** questions in English class.

2 Past tense form. The past tense of regular verbs is formed by adding -*ed* or -*d* to the basic form.

> We **asked** the instructor to postpone the test.
>
> I **named** my son after my grandfather.

3 Present participle. The present participle is the -*ing* form of a verb. It is used in the progressive tenses (see page 9).

> Mimi **is asking** the instructor something in the hallway.
>
> I **am naming** my next child after my grandmother.

4 Past participle. The past participle of a regular verb is the same as its past tense form. The past participle is the form that is used with the helping verbs *have, has,* and *had* and with *am, is, are, was,* or *were.*

Our lab instructors **have asked** us to study in groups.

I **was named** after my mother.

Here are the principal parts of three regular verbs:

Basic Form	Past Tense	Present Participle	Past Participle
work	worked	working	worked
smile	smiled	smiling	smiled
wonder	wondered	wondering	wondered

Irregular verbs, which have irregular forms for the past tense form and past participle, are explained in 6c on pages 10–11.

Six main tenses. The six main tenses in English are present, past, future, present perfect, past perfect, and future perfect. In addition, there is a progressive form of each of those six tenses. Following are more detailed explanations of the tenses.

THE SIMPLE TENSES

Present tense (basic form; add *-s* in the third-person singular). Verbs in the present tense express present action or habitual action. (A habitual action is one that is often repeated.)

The dogs **smell** the neighbor's barbecue.

Smell expresses a present action.

Mick **plays** basketball every Saturday.

Plays expresses a habitual action.

The forms of present tense verbs are shown with the verb *work* in the box below. Notice the difference between the third-person singular and the other present tense forms.

Present Tense Forms

	Singular	Plural
First person	I work	we work
Second person	you work	you work
Third person	he, she, it works	they work

Past tense for regular verbs (basic form + *-ed* or *-d*). Verbs in the past tense express actions that took place in the past.

The town **painted** designs on all of its fire hydrants.

Last night our dog **chased** a raccoon.

Past Tense Forms

Singular	Plural
I, you, he, she, it worked	we, you, they worked

Note: People sometimes drop the *-ed* or *-d* ending in their everyday speech. They then tend to omit those endings in their writing as well. For example, someone might say, "I

finish the paper an hour before class" instead of "I finished the paper an hour before class." In written English, however, the *-ed* or *-d* ending is essential.

Future tense (*will* + basic form). Verbs in the future tense describe future actions.

The dew **will evaporate** by noon.

Future Tense Forms

Singular	Plural
I, you, he, she, it will work	we, you, they will work

THE PERFECT TENSES

The perfect tenses are made up of a form of *have* plus the past participle.

Present perfect tense (*have* or *has* + past participle). The present perfect tense describes an action that began in the past and either has been finished or is continuing at the present time.

I **have taken** five pages of notes on the textbook chapter.

Mr. Alvarez **has known** me all my life.

Here are the present perfect tense forms of *work.* Notice the difference between the third-person singular and the other present perfect tense forms.

Present Perfect Tense Forms

	Singular	Plural
First person	I have worked	we have worked
Second person	you have worked	you have worked
Third person	he, she, it has worked	they have worked

Past perfect tense (*had* + past participle). The past perfect tense describes an action that was completed in the past before another past action.

My neighbor **had watered** all of his tomato plants just before the sudden rainstorm arrived.

Past Perfect Tense Forms

Singular	Plural
I, you, he, she, it had worked	we, you, they had worked

Future perfect tense (*will have* + past participle). The future perfect tense describes an action that will be completed before some time in the future.

By graduation, Arthur **will have sent** out a hundred résumés.

Future Perfect Tense Forms

Singular	Plural
I, you, he, she, it will have worked	we, you, they will have worked

THE PROGRESSIVE TENSES

The **progressive tenses** express actions still in progress at a particular time. The simple progressives—present, past, future progressive tenses—are made by adding a form of the helping verb *be* to the present participle, the *-ing* form of the verb. The perfect progressives—present perfect, past perfect, and future perfect progressive tenses—are made by adding a form of the helping verb *have* plus *been* to the present participle.

Present progressive tense (*am, are,* or *is* + present participle).   The present progressive tense expresses an action taking place at this moment or that will occur sometime in the future.

> You **are acting** strangely.
>
> Jay **is washing** his car now.
>
> I **am going** to get home late tonight.

Present Progressive Tense Forms

	Singular	Plural
First person	I am working	we are working
Second person	you are working	you are working
Third person	he, she, it is working	they are working

Past progressive tense (*was* or *were* + present participle).   The past progressive tense expresses an action that was in progress at a certain time in the past.

> Mr. Austin **was talking** to a client when you called.
>
> Early this morning, geese **were honking** loudly overhead.

Past Progressive Tense Forms

	Singular	Plural
First person	I was working	we were working
Second person	you were working	you were working
Third person	he, she, it was working	they were working

Future progressive tense (*will be* + present participle).   The future progressive tense expresses an action that will be in progress at a certain time in the future.

> A reporter **will be interviewing** the governor this afternoon.

Future Progressive Tense Forms

Singular	Plural
I, you, he, she, it will be working	we, you, they will be working

Note: The *-ing* form of a verb cannot stand by itself as the verb of a sentence—it must be accompanied by a helping verb.

> **Incorrect:** The visitors *pacing* in the hospital lobby.
> **Correct:** The visitors **were pacing** in the hospital lobby.

Present perfect progressive tense (*have been* or *has been* + present participle).   The present perfect progressive tense expresses an ongoing action that began in the past and continues in the present.

> I **have been waiting** for the bus for twenty minutes.
>
> It **has been raining** for days.

Present Perfect Progressive Tense Forms

	Singular	Plural
First person	I have been working	we have been working
Second person	you have been working	you have been working
Third person	he, she, it has been working	they have been working

Past perfect progressive tense (*had been* + present participle).   The past perfect progressive tense expresses an ongoing action that was completed before another action.

> The mayor **had been planning** on running for office again until he became ill.

Past Perfect Progressive Tense Forms

Singular	Plural
I, you, he, she, it had been working	we, you, they had been working

Future perfect progressive tense (*will have been* + present participle).   The future perfect progressive tense expresses an ongoing action that will be completed at some time in the future.

> Next year, Professor Walters **will have been teaching** for forty years.

Future Perfect Progressive Tense Forms

Singular	Plural
I, you, he, she, it will have been working	we, you, they will have been working

Consistent verb tense.   Avoid illogical or needless shifts in tense. For example, if you are writing a paper with the action in the past tense, don't shift suddenly to the present for no reason.

> **Inconsistent verb tense:** Harry *saw* my grade on the chemistry test and then *asks* me to tutor him.

There is no reason for the writer to shift suddenly from the past tense (*saw*) to the present tense (*asks*). The inconsistency can be corrected by using the same tense for both verbs:

> **Consistent verb tense:** Harry **saw** my grade on the chemistry test and then **asked** me to tutor him.

6b   Mood and voice

Correct and consistent use of mood. A verb's **mood** reveals how a writer views a thought or action—as a fact, a question, a wish, and so on. There are three moods: indicative, imperative, and subjunctive.

Use the **indicative mood**—the most common English mood by far—for facts, opinions, and questions of fact.

> Jan **is** majoring in special education.
>
> She **has** made a good choice.
>
> What **is** your major?

Use the **imperative mood** for commands, requests, and advice. Imperative verbs are always in the second person (*you*). The subject, *you*, is understood but not stated.

> **Go** away!
>
> Please **wipe** your shoes off.
>
> **Try** the mushroom soup.

Use the **subjunctive mood** for wishes and in *if* clauses that express desires or conditions contrary to fact. In such cases, use the past tense of the verb. For the verb *be*, the past tense subjunctive is always *were* (not *was*), even for singular subjects.

> I wish Tai **were** here.
>
> It would be nice if you **came** to the meetings
>
> If I **were** Opal, I would look for a more satisfying job.

Also use the subjunctive mood in *that* clauses that express demands, recommendations, or requests. In such cases, use the base form (the dictionary form) of the verb (for example, *be*, *go*, and *buy*).

> The company insists that all employees **be** at work exactly at eight o'clock.
>
> We ask that each worker **go** to the polls today.
>
> The instructor recommends that each student **buy** a good paperback dictionary.

Avoid illogical or needless shifts in mood.

> **Inconsistent mood:** *Read* the chapter, and *you should do* the practices.
>
> > The sentence changes from the imperative mood *(Read the chapter)* to the indicative mood *(you should do . . .)*.
>
> **Consistent mood:** Read the chapter, and **do** the practices.

The passive and active voices. The subject of a sentence usually performs the action of the verb. In such cases, the verb is in the **active voice**. For example, look at the following sentence:

> My father **planted** the Japanese maple tree in the front yard.

The verb in this sentence is *planted*. Who performed that action? The answer is *father*, the subject of the sentence. Therefore, the verb is in the active voice. Now look at this version of that sentence:

> The Japanese maple tree in the front yard **was planted** by my father.

The verb in this sentence is *was planted*. The subject of the sentence, *tree*, did not perform the action. The tree was acted upon by the father. When the subject of a sentence is acted upon, the verb is in the **passive voice**.

Passive verbs are formed by combining a form of *to be* (*am, is, are, was, were*) with the past participle of a verb (which for regular verbs is the same as their past tense form). For example, in the sentence above, *was* plus the past participle of *plant* results in the passive verb *was planted*. Below are some other passive verbs.

Form of to be	+	*past participle*	=	*passive verb*
am	+	pushed	=	am pushed
is	+	surprised	=	is surprised
was	+	delayed	=	was delayed

In general, write in the active voice. Because it expresses action, it is usually more energetic and effective than the passive voice.

> **Active:** Sheila **tossed** an apple to me.
> **Passive:** An apple **was tossed** to me by Sheila.
> > The active version is more lively and direct.

However, use the passive voice when you wish to emphasize the receiver of the action or when the performer of the action is unknown.

> Last week my car **was stolen**.
>
> Telephone orders **are taken** twenty-four hours a day.

6c   Irregular verbs

Most English verbs are **regular**. That is, they form their past tense and past participle by adding *-ed* or *-d* to the basic form, as for *work* (work**ed**) and *smile* (smil**ed**). **Irregular** verbs, however, do not follow that pattern. Instead, their past tense forms and past participles are formed in various ways, as with these two irregular verbs:

Basic Form	*Past Tense Form*	*Past Participle*
hide	hid	hidden
swim	swam	swum

Note: The present participle of both regular and irregular verbs is formed simply by adding *-ing* to the basic form (sometimes with minor spelling variations): *working, smiling, hiding, swimming*.

On the next page are some of the most common irregular verbs. Review them enough to become familiar with them. When deciding on whether to use the past tense form or the past participle, keep in mind these points:

- If a sentence does not include a helping verb, choose the past tense form.

- If the sentence includes a helping verb, choose the past participle.

Common Irregular Verbs

Basic Form	Past Tense Form	Past Participle
be (am, are, is)	was, were	been
become	became	become
begin	began	begun
blow	blew	blown
break	broke	broken
bring	brought	brought
catch	caught	caught
choose	chose	chosen
come	came	come
cut	cut	cut
do	did	done
draw	drew	drawn
drink	drank	drunk
drive	drove	driven
eat	ate	eaten
fall	fell	fallen
feel	felt	felt
find	found	found
fly	flew	flown
freeze	froze	frozen
get	got	got, gotten
give	gave	given
go	went	gone
grow	grew	grown
have	had, has	had
hide	hid	hidden
keep	kept	kept
know	knew	known
lay (put)	laid	laid
leave	left	left
lend	lent	lent
lie (recline)	lay	lain
lose	lost	lost
make	made	made
read	read	read
ride	rode	ridden
rise	rose	risen
run	ran	run
say	said	said
see	saw	seen
sell	sold	sold
set (place)	set	set
shake	shook	shaken
sit (take a seat)	sat	sat
sleep	slept	slept
speak	spoke	spoken
spend	spent	spent
steal	stole	stolen
stink	stank, stunk	stunk
swim	swam	swum
take	took	taken
teach	taught	taught
tell	told	told
think	thought	thought
throw	threw	thrown
wear	wore	worn
win	won	won
write	wrote	written

If you think a verb is irregular and it is not in the above list, look it up in your dictionary. If it is irregular, the principal parts will be listed.

6d   Subject-verb agreement

In a correctly written sentence, the subject and verb **agree** (match) in number. Singular subjects have singular verbs, and plural subjects have plural verbs.

In simple sentences of few words, it's not difficult to make the subject and verb agree:

Our *baby* **sleeps** more than ten hours a day. Some *babies* **sleep** even longer.

However, not all sentences are as straightforward as the above examples. This section will explain situations that can cause problems with subject-verb agreement.

Words between subject and verb. A verb often comes right after its subject.

The sealed *boxes* **belong** to my brother.

(Here and in the rest of the section, the subject is shown in *italic* type, and the verb is shown in **boldface** type.)

However, at times the subject and verb are separated by other words. In such cases, be sure that the verb agrees with the subject, not one of the in-between words. For instance, the subject and verb often have a prepositional phrase between them. A prepositional phrase begins with a preposition and ends with a noun or pronoun. *In, on, for, from, of, to* and *by* are common prepositions. (A longer list of prepositions is on page 3.)

The sealed *boxes* under the bed **belong** to my brother.

This subject and verb are separated by the prepositional phrase *under the bed*. The verb must agree with the subject, *boxes*, not with *bed*.

The *tomatoes* in this salad **are** brown and mushy.

Because the subject, *tomatoes*, is plural, the verb must also be plural. The prepositional phrase, *in this salad*, has no effect on the subject and verb agreement.

Note: Phrases that begin with such words as *as well as, along with, together with,* and *in addition to* do not make a singular subject plural: My *mother*, as well as her sister, **speaks** Japanese. A fax *machine*, along with a computer, **is** useful in a home office.

Verb before the subject. The verb follows the subject in most sentences: *Hank* **passed** the course. The *plane* **roared** overhead.

However, in some sentences, the verb comes before the subject. To make the subject and verb agree in such cases, look for the subject after the verb. Then decide if the verb should be singular or plural. The verb will always come first in sentences that begin with such words as *there is* or *here are*.

There **are** *mice* in the basement.

Because the subject of this sentence (*mice*) is plural, the verb (*are*) should be plural as well.

Here **is** the *menu*.

The subject of this sentence is *menu*, which needs a singular verb.

The verb may also come first in questions or sentences that begin with prepositional phrases.

What **was** your *score* on the test?

> The verb *was* is singular. It agrees with the singular subject *score*. *On the test* is a prepositional phrase. The subject of a sentence is never in a prepositional phrase.

On that shelf **are** the *reports* for this year.

> The sentence begins with the prepositional phrase *on that shelf*, which is followed by the plural verb *are*. You can find the subject by asking, "What are on that shelf?" The answer is the subject of the sentence: *reports*.

Note: The subject may be easier to find if you rearrange the sentence so the subject comes first. For the sentences above, you would then get the following: *Mice* **are** in the basement. The *menu* **is** here. Your *score* on the test **was** what? The *reports* for this year **are** on that shelf.

Linking verbs. A linking verb may join the subject to a noun or pronoun that describes the subject. Be sure the verb agrees with its subject, not with the noun or pronoun that follows the verb.

The last *item* on the menu **is** special coffees.

> The linking verb must agree with the singular subject, *item*, not with the plural noun *coffees*.

Special *coffees* **are** the last item on the menu.

> The verb must agree with the subject, *coffees*, not with *item*.

Special singular and plural subjects

Compound subjects. A compound subject is made up of two nouns connected by a coordinating conjunction. Subjects joined by *and* generally take a plural verb.

Running and *weightlifting* **are** good ways to keep in shape.

Fear and *ignorance* **have** a lot to do with hatred.

Exception: When the subjects refer to one person or thing, use a singular verb: The *vice president and general manager* [one person] **is** out of town. *Chips and dip* [one snack] **is** one of my favorite snacks.

However, when a compound subject is connected by *or, nor, either . . . or,* or *neither . . . nor,* the verb must agree with the part of the subject that is closer to it.

A *cup* of coffee or a *glass* of soda **is** always on Ken's desk.

Either *he* or his *parents* **were** home that night.

Note: Since it sounds more natural to use a plural verb in sentences with compound subjects, most writers would put the plural subject second, as above.

Collective nouns. A collective noun refers to persons or things that are generally thought of as one unit. Following are some examples:

Collective Nouns

audience	committee	group	quartet
band	couple	herd	society
class	family	jury	team

Collective nouns are considered singular unless they specifically refer to members of the group as individuals.

The *family* **lives** on Russell Avenue.

> *Family* refers to a single unit, so the singular verb *lives* is used.

The *family* **are** Republicans, Democrats, and Independents.

> Since one unit cannot have three different political views, *family* in this sentence clearly refers to the individual members of the group, so the plural verb *are* is used.

Note: To emphasize the individuals in the example sentence above, some writers would use a subject that is clearly plural: The *members* of the family **are** Republicans, Democrats, and Independents.

Indefinite pronoun subjects. Indefinite pronouns are pronouns that do not refer to a specific person or thing. The ones in the box below are always singular.

Singular Indefinite Pronouns

each	anyone	anybody	anything
either	everyone	everybody	everything
neither	someone	somebody	something
one	no one	nobody	nothing

Each of the puppies **is** cute in its own way.

Neither of the girls **knows** her Social Security number.

Despite the rules, nearly *everyone* in my apartment building **owns** a pet.

The following indefinite pronouns are always plural:

Plural Indefinite Pronouns

both	many	several
few	others	

Both of the puppies **are** cute in their own ways.

The following indefinite pronouns are singular or plural, depending on their context:

Indefinite Pronouns That Can Be Singular or Plural

all	more	none
any	most	some

Most of her outfit **is** white.

> *Most* here refers to one thing—the outfit, so the singular verb *is* is used.

Most of the salespeople **are** friendly.

> *Most* here refers to several salespeople, so the plural verb *are* is used.

Relative pronoun subjects: *who, which, that*. The relative pronouns *who, which,* and *that* are singular when they refer to a singular noun. They are plural when they refer to a plural noun.

Elaine bought a used T-shirt *that* **looks** brand-new.

Elaine bought two used T-shirts *that* **look** brand-new.

When a phrase begins with the words *one of the*, use a plural verb for the relative pronoun that follows.

Ramon is one of the students *who* **volunteer** at the local nursing home.

Who refers to *students*, so a plural verb is needed.

When a phrase begins with the words *the only one of the*, use a singular verb for the relative pronoun that follows.

He is the only one of the students *who* **speaks** Spanish.

In this case, *who* refers to *one*, so a singular verb is used.

Singular subjects with a plural form. Some nouns with a plural form often have singular meanings. Examples include *athletics, mathematics, politics,* and *mumps.* When used with a singular meaning, such nouns take singular verbs.

Mathematics **is** Yuri's favorite subject.

Exceptions: Some words ending in *s* that refer to two-part things—such as *pants, trousers,* and *eyeglasses*—need a plural verb: My *eyeglasses* often **slip** down my nose. If you're unsure about whether a word takes a singular or a plural verb, check a dictionary.

Titles and words used as words. Titles of works and words used as words are singular.

Little Women **remains** popular more than a century after it was written.

The subject is the book (singular), not the women (plural).

Appendixes **is** the preferred plural of *appendix.*

The subject is the singular word *appendixes*, not two or more appendixes.

Amounts and measurements. When an amount or measurement is referred to as a single thing, use a singular verb.

These days, five *dollars* **gets** you a ticket to the movies and no popcorn.

One-half of the yard **is** mowed.

When the items that make up the amount are referred to as separate parts, use a plural verb.

The *dollars* **are** stuffed into an old pickle jar.

Two-thirds of the students **have** given their speeches.

The word *number* takes a singular verb when it is preceded by *the*; it takes a plural verb when preceded by *a.*

The *number* of unemployed workers **is** down.

A *number* of workers in our office **were** laid off.

7 / Pronouns

7a   Pronoun case

Depending on their use in a sentence, pronouns have different **cases**, or forms: the subjective, objective, and possessive cases.

Subjective case. Pronouns in the subjective case act as the subjects of verbs or, after linking verbs, as subject complements. Here are the subjective forms of personal pronouns.

Subjective Case

	First Person	Second Person	Third Person
Singular	I	you	he, she, it
Plural	we	you	they

She always brings her lunch to work.

She is the subject of the verb *brings.*

The person in charge is **he**.

He is the complement of the subject, *person.*

Objective case. Pronouns in the objective case act as the objects of verbs or of prepositions. Here is a list of the objective forms of personal pronouns.

Objective Case

	First Person	Second Person	Third Person
Singular	me	you	him, her, it
Plural	us	you	them

When a pronoun is a direct or an indirect object, use the objective form.

The cat scratched **her**.

Her is the direct object of the verb *scratched. Her* tells who was scratched.

Flo knitted **him** a tie.

Him is the indirect object of the verb *knitted. Him* tells for whom the tie was knitted.

When a pronoun is the object of a preposition, use the objective form. Prepositions are words such as *to, for, of,* and *from.* (A longer list of prepositions is on page 3.)

My sister tossed the car keys to **me**.

Me is the object of the preposition *to.*

Possessive case. Pronouns in the possessive case show that something is owned, or possessed. Here are the possessive forms of personal pronouns.

Possessive Case

	First Person	Second Person	Third Person
Singular	my, mine	your, yours	his, her, hers, its
Plural	our, ours	your, yours	their, theirs

Neal and Emily saw many of **their** friends at the party.

Their friends means *the friends belonging to Neal and Emily.*

If Gordon needs a sweater, he can borrow **mine**.

Mine means *the sweater belonging to me.* Note that in cases in which the pronoun is not followed by a noun, the form *mine, yours, his, hers, ours,* or *theirs* is used.

Note: Possessive pronouns never contain an apostrophe: During the last storm, our apple tree lost all of **its** blossoms [not *its'* blossoms].

7b   Pronoun usage

Pronouns with *and* and *or*. Deciding which pronoun to use may become confusing when there are compound subjects or objects (that is, more than one subject or object) joined by *and* or *or*. However, the rules remain the same: Use the subjective case for the subject of a verb; use the objective case for the object of a verb or preposition.

My brother and **I** loved the Wizard of Oz books.

> *I* is a subject of the verb *loved. Brother* is also a subject of *loved.*

Our parents often read to my brother and **me**.

> *Me* is an object of the preposition *to. Brother* is also an object of *to.*

You can figure out which pronoun to use by mentally leaving out the other word that goes with *and* or *or*. For instance, in the first example above, omitting the words *my brother and* makes it clear that *I* is the correct pronoun to use: . . . **I** loved the Wizard of Oz books. (You would never say, "*Me* loved the Wizard of Oz books.")

Pronouns in comparisons. When pronouns are used in comparisons, they often follow the word *than* or *as*.

My roommate, Matt, wakes up earlier than **I**.
Rhonda's behavior puzzled you as much as **me**.

Words are often omitted in comparisons. To see whether you should use a subject or an object pronoun, mentally fill in the missing words. In the first sentence above, *I* is the subject of the understood verb *do*.

My roommate, Matt, wakes up earlier than **I** [do].

In the second sentence, *me* is the object of the verb *puzzled*. That verb is understood but not stated for the second part of the comparison.

Rhonda's behavior puzzled you as much as [it puzzled] **me**.

Who and whom in dependent clauses. *Who* is a subject pronoun; *whom* is an object pronoun. Choose one of these pronouns based on its function in a dependent clause.

The person **who** owns the expensive car won't let anybody else park it.

> *Who owns the expensive car* is a dependent clause. *Who* is the subject of the verb *owns.*

The babysitter **whom** they trust cannot work tonight.

> *Whom they trust* is a dependent clause. *Whom* is the object of the verb *trust*. The subject of *trust* is *they.*

As a general rule, to know which of the two words to use, find the first verb after *who* or *whom*. Decide whether that verb already has a subject. If it doesn't have a subject, use the subject pronoun *who*. If it does have a subject, use the object pronoun *whom*.

Don't be confused when words such as *I think* or *we believe* intervene. When a dependent clause contains such an expression, mentally omit the expression before deciding between *who* and *whom*.

Professor Bell is the person **who** I believe is head of the English department.

> *Who* is the subject of the verb *is. I* is the subject of the verb *believe.*

Who and whom in questions. In questions, *who* is a subject pronoun, and *whom* is an object pronoun. You can often decide whether to use *who* or *whom* in a question in the same way you decide to use those words in clauses. (See the previous section.)

Who should go?

> The verb after *who* is *should go*, which does not have another subject. Therefore, use the subject form of the pronoun, *who.*

Whom should I hire?

> *I* is the subject of the verb *should hire*, so use the object form of the pronoun, *whom (I should hire whom?).*

Pronoun appositives. An **appositive** renames a noun or pronoun, identifying it in some way. When the appositive is a pronoun, it has the same function within a sentence as the noun or pronoun it renames.

Incorrect: The coaches, Hana and *me*, tried to raise money for uniforms.
Correct: The coaches, Hana and **I**, tried to raise money for uniforms.

> Since *coaches* is the subject of the sentence, the appositive must be in the subjective case.

Incorrect: The tutor worked at the same time with both students, Ravi and *I*.
Correct: The tutor worked at the same time with both students, Ravi and **me**.

> Since *students* is the object of the preposition *with*, the appositive must be in the objective case.

We or us followed by a noun. If the pronoun functions as the subject of the sentence, use *we*. If the pronoun serves as an object, use *us*. You may find it easier to choose the pronoun by imagining that the noun after *we* or *us* is not there.

Incorrect: *Us* gardeners can't wait for spring.
Correct: **We** gardeners can't wait for spring.

> If *gardeners* were removed, then the sentence would be *We can't wait for spring* (not *Us can't wait for spring*).

Incorrect: Seed catalogues inspire *we* gardeners throughout the winter.
Correct: Seed catalogues inspire **us** gardeners throughout the winter.

> If *gardeners* were removed, the sentence would be *Seed catalogues inspire us throughout the winter* [not *Seed catalogues inspire we throughout the winter*].

Pronouns in infinitive phrases. An **infinitive** is *to* followed by a verb (for example, *to work* or *to speak*). Use objective pronouns as both subjects and objects of infinitives.

Kareem asked **me** to drive **him** to work tomorrow.

> *Me* is the subject and *him* is the object of the infinitive *to drive.*

Pronouns before a gerund. A **gerund** is the -ing form of a verb functioning as a noun: **Laughing** can be therapeutic. Use the possessive case of a pronoun that is followed by a gerund.

> **Incorrect:** *Me* leaving was a problem for my boss.
> **Correct:** **My** leaving was a problem for my boss.
>
> **Incorrect:** The instructor was pleased with *us* handing in all the papers on time.
> **Correct:** The instructor was pleased with **our** handing in all the papers on time.

7c Pronoun-antecedent agreement

Pronoun agreement in number. A pronoun must agree in number with its **antecedent**, the noun or pronoun it refers to. Singular antecedents require singular pronouns; plural antecedents require plural pronouns.

(In the examples, pronouns are printed in **boldface** type; antecedents are printed in *italic* type.)

> **Singular:** The dying *tree* lost all **its** leaves.
> **Plural:** Do the *neighbors* know that **their** dog is loose?
> **Plural:** *Linda and Ted* act like newlyweds, but **they** have been married for years.
>
> When a pronoun refers to antecedents joined by *and*, use a plural pronoun.

Indefinite pronouns. Unlike other pronouns, indefinite pronouns do not refer to particular persons or things. The following indefinite pronouns are always singular:

Singular Indefinite Pronouns

each	anyone	anybody	anything
either	everyone	everybody	everything
neither	someone	somebody	something
one	no one	nobody	nothing

> *Something* has left **its** muddy footprints on the hood of the car.
> *One* of my sisters has lost **her** job.
> *Everybody* is entitled to change **his or her** mind.
>
> **Note on gender agreement:** Choose a pronoun that agrees in gender with its antecedent. The clearly feminine antecedent *one of my sisters* is correctly referred to with *her*. However, *everybody* includes males and females, so it should be referred to with *his or her*. If *his or her* seems awkward, rewrite the sentence with a plural subject: *People* are entitled to change **their** minds.

The following indefinite pronouns are always plural:

Plural Indefinite Pronouns

both	many	several
few	others	

> *Both* of my brothers worked **their** way through college.

The following indefinite pronouns are singular or plural, depending on their context:

Indefinite Pronouns That Can Be Singular or Plural

all	more	none
any	most	some

> *Some* of the pie is fine, but **its** crust is burnt.
>> *Some* here refers to one thing, the pie, so the singular pronoun *its* is used.
>
> *Some* of the students forgot **their** books.
>> *Some* here refers to several students, so the plural pronoun *their* is used.

Antecedents that are joined by *or* or *nor*. When antecedents are joined by *or* or *nor*, the pronoun should agree with the nearer antecedent.

> Either Judith or *Ivy* will give **her** speech in class today.
> Neither the coach nor the *parents* will get **their** way.
>
> **Note:** Since it would sound odd to use a singular pronoun in sentences like the second example, most writers would put the plural antecedent second, as above.

Collective nouns. A collective noun refers to a group of persons or things. Collective nouns are singular when they refer to the group, not the individuals.

Some Collective Nouns

audience	committee	group	quartet
band	couple	herd	society
class	family	jury	team

> The *class* voted to take **its** final exam early.

However, if a collective noun refers to the individual members of the group, a plural pronoun is used.

> The *class* handed in **their** essays before vacation.

Many writers feel it is awkward to use a collective noun as a plural. They prefer to revise the sentence.

> The class *members* handed in **their** essays before vacation.

Pronoun agreement in person. A pronoun that refers to the speaker, such as *I* or *our*, is called a **first-person pronoun**. A pronoun that refers to someone being spoken to, such as *you*, is a **second-person pronoun**. And a pronoun that refers to another person or thing, such as *he* or *it*, is a **third-person pronoun**.

Following are the personal pronouns in first-, second-, and third-person groupings:

Personal Pronouns

	First person	Second person	Third person
Singular	I, me, my, mine	you, your, yours	he, him, his; she, her, hers; it, its
Plural	we, us, our, ours	you, your, yours	they, them, their, theirs

Pronouns must agree in person with their antecedents. The sentences below, for example, show some needless shifts in person.

Incorrect: The worst thing about *my* not writing letters is that *you* never get any back.

Incorrect: Although *we* like most of *our* neighbors, there are a few *you* can't get along with.

These sentences begin with first-person pronouns (*my, we* and *our*) but then shift unnecessarily to the second-person pronoun *you*. In academic writing, use *you* to refer only to the reader.

Correct: The worst thing about *my* not writing letters is that **I** never get any back.

Correct: Though *we* like most of *our* neighbors, there are a few **we** can't get along with.

7d   Clear pronoun reference

A pronoun must refer clearly to its antecedent, the word or words it stands for. If a pronoun's antecedent is uncertain, the sentence will be confusing. Pronouns will be unclear if they have two possible antecedents or no clearly stated antecedent.

Avoiding two or more possible antecedents.   A pronoun's reference will not be clear if there are two or more possible antecedents.

Incorrect: Eva told her mother that *she* had received a postcard from Alaska.

Who received the letter, Eva or her mother?

Incorrect: I wrote a to-do list with my purple pen, and now I can't find *it*.

What can't the writer find, the list or the pen?

Be especially careful with *this, that*, and *which*. They are commonly used to refer vaguely to previously stated ideas.

Incorrect: Many people moved years ago to big homes in the suburbs with big lawns, *which* have become hard for their now elderly owners to care for.

What have become hard for the elderly owners to care for—the big homes, the big lawns, or both?

An unclear sentence with two antecedents can sometimes be corrected by using the speaker's exact words.

Correct: Eva told her mother, "**I** received [*or* "**You** received] a postcard from Alaska."

In other cases, the best solution is to replace the pronoun with the word or words it was meant to refer to.

Correct: I wrote a to-do list with my purple pen, and now I can't find **the list** [*or* **the pen**].

Correct: Many people moved years ago to big homes in the suburbs with big lawns, **both of which** have become hard for their now elderly owners to care for.

Avoiding no antecedent.   A pronoun's reference will not be clear if its antecedent is missing.

Incorrect: I just received our cable TV bill. *They* said the Disney Channel is providing a free preview next month.

Who said there's a free preview? We don't know because *they* has no word to refer to.

Incorrect: My older brother is a chemist, but *that* doesn't interest me.

The pronoun *that* is meant to refer to the implied subject *chemistry*, but a pronoun must have a named antecedent, not an implied one.

To correct an unclear reference in which a pronoun has no antecedent, replace the pronoun with the word or words it is meant to refer to.

Correct: I just received our cable TV bill. **The cable company** said the Disney Channel is providing a free preview next month.

Correct: My older brother is a chemist, but **chemistry** doesn't interest me.

Keep in mind that possessives and other modifiers cannot serve as antecedents.

Incorrect: William Henry Harrison's presidency was the shortest in American history. *He* died in 1841 after being in office for only thirty-one days.

He has no word to refer to—it cannot refer to the possessive *William Henry Harrison's*.

Correct: William Henry Harrison's presidency was the shortest in American history. **Harrison** died in 1841 after being in office for only thirty-one days.

8 / Adjectives and Adverbs

An **adjective** modifies (describes) a noun or pronoun. It usually comes before the noun or pronoun it modifies and explains such things as what kind, which one, and how many. An adjective that modifies the subject of a sentence may also come after a linking verb (such as *is, be, were, seem*, and *smell*).

The **weary** hikers shuffled down the **dusty** road.

The adjectives *weary* and *dusty* describe the nouns that follow them.

The flowers smell **sweet**.

The adjective *sweet* follows the linking verb *smell* and describes the subject, *flowers*.

An **adverb** is a word that modifies a verb, an adjective, or another adverb. Adverbs generally explain such things as how, when, where, why, and how much. While many adverbs end in *-ly*, not all do (run **fast**, run **late**, run **more**).

The chef **carefully** spread raspberry frosting over the cake.

The adverb *carefully* modifies the verb *spread*.

Ann was **extremely** embarrassed when she stumbled on stage.

The adverb *extremely* modifies the adjective *embarrassed*.

That lamp shines **very brightly**.

The adverb *very* modifies the adverb *brightly*. *Brightly* modifies the verb *shines*.

Be careful to use an adverb—not an adjective—to modify an action verb.

Incorrect: Rajit snored *loud* at his desk.
Correct: Rajit snored **loudly** at his desk.

Some verbs—such as *look, sound, smell, feel,* and *taste*—can function as either linking or action verbs.

Incorrect: The child smelled the flowers *enthusiastic*.
Correct: The child smelled the flowers **enthusiastically**.

Smelled in this case is an action verb—it tells what the child did. Therefore, the modifier describes the verb, not the subject, so an adverb is needed.

8a   Using adjectives and adverbs in comparisons

To compare two persons or things, add *-er* to most adjectives of one and two syllables and to adverbs of one syllable. For longer adjectives and adverbs, do not add *-er*. Instead, add the word *more*.

Grilling food is **faster** than roasting.

My dog is **more intelligent** than my cat.

To compare three or more persons or things, add *-est* to most adjectives of one and two syllables and to adverbs of one syllable. For longer adjectives and adverbs, do not add *-est*. Instead, add the word *most*.

Grilling food is faster than roasting, but microwaving is **fastest** of all.

My dog is more intelligent than my cat, but my parrot is the **most intelligent** pet I have ever had.

Note: Do not use both an *-er* ending and *more*, or an *-est* ending and *most*: One twin's hair is ~~more~~ **curlier** than the other's.

Irregular adjective and adverb forms. Certain short adjectives and adverbs have irregular forms:

	Comparing two	Comparing three or more
bad, badly	worse	worst
good, well	better	best
little	less	least
much, many	more	most

Sid is doing **badly** in speech class, but I'm doing even **worse**.
The grape cough syrup tastes **better** than the orange syrup, but the lemon cough drops taste the **best**.

8b   Using two troublesome pairs: *good* and *well, bad* and *badly*

Good is an adjective that often means "enjoyable," "talented," or "positive": I had a **good** day. Sue is a **good** skier. Think **good** thoughts.
Bad is an adjective; *badly* is an adverb: I feel **bad**. I need sleep **badly**.
As an adverb, *well* often means "skillfully" or "successfully": Sue skis **well**. The schedule worked **well**. Pedro interacts **well** with others.
As an adjective, *well* means "healthy": The patient is **well** once again.

8c   Avoiding double negatives

In standard English, it is incorrect to express a negative idea by pairing one negative with another. Common negative words include *not, nothing, never, nowhere, nobody,* and *neither*. To correct a double negative, either eliminate one of the negative words or replace a negative with a positive word.

Incorrect: I *shouldn't* go *nowhere* this weekend.
Correct: I **should** go nowhere this weekend.
Correct: I shouldn't go **anywhere** this weekend.

The words *hardly, scarcely,* and *barely* are also negatives. They should not be paired with other negatives, such as *never* and *not*. Correct a double negative containing *hardly, scarcely,* or *barely* by eliminating the other negative word.

Incorrect: I *couldn't hardly* recognize you.
Correct: I **could** hardly recognize you.

9 / Fragments

A **fragment** is a part of a sentence that is punctuated as if it were a complete sentence. Following are several common types of sentence fragments and ways to correct them.

9a Dependent-clause fragments

A dependent clause begins with a word such as *after, because, if, since, when, who,* and *which* that keeps the clause from being able to stand on its own as a sentence. (Dependent clauses are explained further in 4b, page 6.)

To keep a dependent clause from being a fragment, connect it to a sentence that comes before or after it.

> **Fragment:** *After he turned off the television set.* Tomas picked up a book.
> **Revision:** After he turned off the television set**,** Tomas picked up a book.

> **Fragment:** I had to break a window. *Since I had lost my house key.*
> **Revision:** I had to break a window **since** I had lost my house key.

> **Fragment:** Yesterday my wife ran into a fellow. *Who had been her best friend in high school.*
> **Revision:** Yesterday my wife ran into a fellow **who** had been her best friend in high school.

> **Punctuation note:** A dependent clause that begins a sentence should generally be followed by a comma. (See 16b, page 26.)

9b Fragments without a subject

Some fragments have a verb, but lack a subject. A word group without a subject is not a complete sentence. Such a fragment can be corrected in two ways: 1) Connect it to the sentence that comes before it. 2) Create a new sentence by adding a subject to the fragment.

> **Fragment:** The landlord unclogged the drain. *And found a dishcloth stuck in the pipe.*
>> In the second word group, the verb *found* has no subject.

> **Revision:** The landlord unclogged the drain **and** found a dishcloth stuck in the pipe.
>> The first clause now has one subject (*landlord*) and two verbs (*unclogged* and *found*).

> **Revision:** The landlord unclogged the drain. **She** found a dishcloth stuck in the pipe.
>> The fragment has been changed to a sentence with the addition of the subject *she*.

9c Fragments without a subject and a verb

-ing **and** ***to*** **fragments.** When *-ing* or *to* appears at or near the beginning of a phrase, a fragment may result. There are two ways to correct *-ing* and *to* fragments: 1) Connect the fragment to the sentence that comes before or after it. 2) Create a complete sentence by adding a subject and a verb to the fragment. To do so,

revise the material as necessary. When an *-ing* or *to* word group starts a sentence, follow it with a comma.

> **Fragment:** *Hoping to furnish their new home cheaply.* The newlyweds often go to garage sales.
> **Revision:** Hoping to furnish their new home cheaply**, the** newlyweds often go to garage sales.
>> The fragment has been added to the sentence that follows it.

> **Fragment:** Lee jogged through the park. *To clear her mind before the midterm.*
> **Revision:** Lee jogged through the park. **She wanted to** clear her mind before the midterm.
>> The fragment has been rewritten to include a subject (*she*) and a verb (*wanted*).

Example and list fragments. Another common type of fragment without a subject or a verb may begin with a word or words like *including, such as, especially, for example,* or *for instance.* This type of fragment is often best corrected by attaching it to the sentence that comes before it.

> **Example fragment:** Most English words come from other languages. *Including German, Latin, and Greek.*
> **Revision:** Most English words come from other languages**, including** German, Latin, and Greek.

A fragment may also be made up of a list of items that is not preceded by an example word.

> **List fragment:** A poll revealed three things Americans most fear. *Speaking before a group, heights, and insects.*
> **Revision:** A poll revealed three things Americans most fear: **speaking** before a group, heights, and insects.
>> The list fragment has been joined to the sentence before it with a colon.

Appositive fragments. An **appositive** is a word or word group that renames a noun or pronoun, identifying it in some way. It is not a complete sentence. Usually the best way to correct an appositive fragment is to use a comma to add it to the sentence that comes before it.

> **Fragment:** The bookstore is owned by Louise Mason. *A spunky seventy-year-old woman.*
> **Revision:** The bookstore is owned by Louise Mason**, a** spunky seventy-year-old woman.

9d Fragments for emphasis and for realistic dialogue

Occasionally a sentence fragment may be used deliberately for emphasis.

> Should the city put more police officers on the streets? **Definitely yes!**

Since we frequently use fragments in conversation, fragments are also useful for adding realism to dialogue.

> "Last night, I found the ring I had lost."
> **"Wonderful. Where?"**
> "In the garbage disposal."
> **"No kidding."**

10 / Fused Sentences and Comma Splices

10a Fused sentences

A **fused sentence** is made up of two independent clauses that are incorrectly joined without a connection between them. (To review independent clauses, see 4a, page 6.) Fused sentences are also known as **run-together sentences** and **run-on sentences**.

> **Fused sentence:** Dolphins have killed sharks they never attack humans.
>
>> The independent clauses are *dolphins have killed sharks* and *they never attack humans*.

10b Comma splices

A **comma splice** is made up of two independent clauses that are incorrectly joined (or spliced) together with only a comma. A comma alone is not enough to connect two independent clauses.

> **Comma splice:** Dolphins have killed sharks, they never attack humans.

10c Correcting fused sentences and comma splices

There are four main ways to correct fused sentences and comma splices.

Method 1: Use a period and a capital letter. Put each independent clause into its own sentence.

> **Fused sentence:** The computer hummed loudly the sound was annoying.
> **Comma splice:** The computer hummed loudly, the sound was annoying.
> **Revision:** The computer hummed loudly. **The** sound was annoying.

Method 2: Use a comma and a coordinating conjunction. Connect two independent clauses into one sentence with a comma and a coordinating conjunction. The most common coordinating conjunctions are *and, but*, and *so*. The others are *or, nor, for*, and *yet*.

> **Fused sentence:** Dolphins have killed sharks they never attack humans.
> **Comma splice:** Dolphins have killed sharks, they never attack humans.
> **Revision:** Dolphins have killed sharks, **but** they never attack humans.

Method 3: Change one of the independent clauses to a dependent one. Make one of the independent clauses dependent by beginning it with a word such as *although, because, since* or *who, which, that*. (For a more complete list of these words, see the subordinating conjunctions on page 4 and the relative pronouns on page 1.) The sentence will then have one dependent clause and one independent clause. When a dependent clause begins a sentence, it generally should be followed by a comma.

> **Fused sentence:** The roads are covered with ice school has been cancelled.
> **Comma splice:** The roads are covered with ice, school has been cancelled.
> **Revision:** **Because** the roads are covered with ice, school has been cancelled.

Method 4: Use a semicolon. Put a semicolon between the two independent clauses. This method is appropriate when the independent clauses are closely related and their relationship is clear without a subordinating word.

> **Fused sentence:** The fish was served with its head still on Jesse quickly lost his appetite.
> **Comma splice:** The fish was served with its head still on, Jesse quickly lost his appetite.
> **Revision:** The fish was served with its head still on; Jesse quickly lost his appetite.

Use a semicolon with a transitional expression. A semicolon can also be used with a transitional expression—such as *however, also, consequently, for example*, or *as a result*—to join two independent clauses. (For a more complete list of transitional expressions, see page 29.) When a transitional expression begins an independent clause, it is generally followed by a comma.

> **Revision:** The fish was served with its head still on; **as a result,** Jesse quickly lost his appetite.

Note: Transitional expressions do not have to introduce an independent clause. They can also be used at other points within a clause, generally set off by commas: The fish was served with its head still on; Jesse, **as a result,** quickly lost his appetite.

11 / Misplaced and Dangling Modifiers

A **modifier** is one or more words that describe other words. Two common errors involving these descriptive words are misplaced modifiers and dangling modifiers.

11a Misplaced modifiers

A **misplaced modifier** is a modifier that is incorrectly separated from the word or words that it describes. In general, keep modifiers and the words they describe as close as possible to each other so that their relationship is clear.

One-word limiting modifiers. A word such as *almost, only, nearly*, and *even* usually must be placed in front of the word it limits. Otherwise, the sentence will convey an unintended meaning.

> **Misplaced modifier:** Kwan *almost* sneezed fifteen times last evening.
> **Revision:** Kwan sneezed **almost** fifteen times last evening.
>
>> Readers of the first sentence might think Kwan almost sneezed fifteen times but in fact did not sneeze at all. To prevent confusion, put *almost* in front of the word it modifies, *fifteen*.

Squinting modifiers. A squinting modifier seems to modify both the word before it and the word after it, leaving the reader unsure about which is meant. Put a squinting modifier in a place where its meaning is clear.

> **Squinting modifier:** The soprano who performed at the choir audition *confidently* looked forward to being chosen as a soloist.
> **Revision:** The soprano who performed **confidently** at the choir audition looked forward to being chosen as a soloist.

Revision: The soprano who performed at the choir audition looked forward **confidently** to being chosen as a soloist.

> The word *confidently* must be placed so the reader knows whether the soprano was confident about performing or about being chosen as a soloist.

Misplaced phrases or clauses. A misplaced phrase or clause confuses readers by seeming to modify a word the author did not intend it to describe. In general, the solution is to place the modifier as close as possible to the word or words it describes.

> **Misplaced phrase:** Sam bought a used car from a local dealer *with a smoky tailpipe*.
> **Revision:** Sam bought a used **car with a smoky tailpipe** from a local dealer.
>
> > The phrase *with a smoky tailpipe* is meant to modify the word *car*, not *dealer*.
>
> **Misplaced clause:** Take this note to Mr. Henderson's office *that Kim wrote*.
> **Revision:** Take this **note that Kim wrote** to Mr. Henderson's office.
>
> > The clause *that Kim wrote* is meant to modify the word *note*, not *office*.

Split infinitives. A split infinitive occurs when the two parts of an infinitive (*to* plus the base form of a verb—*to swim, to imagine*) are separated by a modifier. Often, a split infinitive sounds natural and is clear: *to truly believe, to actually win*. However, when a split infinitive is awkward or confusing, move the modifier to another place in the sentence.

> **Awkward split infinitive:** It is possible *to* each March or April *see* whale sharks by the hundreds on the coast of Western Australia.
> **Revision:** It is possible each March or April **to see** whale sharks by the hundreds on the coast of Western Australia.

11b   Dangling modifiers

A **dangling modifier** has no word in a sentence to logically modify. Dangling modifiers are usually phrases that begin a sentence. When a modifier begins a sentence, it must be followed by the word or words it is meant to describe. There are two methods of correcting a dangling modifier: 1) Follow the modifier with the word or words it is meant to modify. 2) Add a subject and verb to the modifier.

> **Dangling modifier:** *Depressed and disappointed*, running away seemed the only thing for me to do.
> **Revision:** Depressed and disappointed, **I felt that** running away **was** the only thing for me to do.
>
> > The modifier *depressed and disappointed* is meant to describe the word *I*, which is missing in the first sentence.
>
> **Dangling modifier:** *Sitting in the dentist's chair*, the sound of the drill awakened Larry's old fears.
> **Revision:** **As Larry sat** in the dentist's chair, the sound of the drill awakened **his** old fears.

> > The modifier *sitting in the dentist's chair* is meant to describe *Larry*, which is absent in the first sentence. The problem can be solved by adding to the modifier a subject (*Larry*) and a verb (*sat*).

12 / Parallelism

At times, you will need to present two or more equal ideas in a sentence. You must then be careful to present the ideas in matching form. This matching form is called **parallelism**.

> **Not parallel:** Dinner consisted of broiled chicken, baked potatoes, and *broccoli that was steamed*.

All of the items in the list of foods play an equal role in the sentence, so they should be expressed in parallel form. *Broiled chicken* and *baked potatoes* are parallel. The adjectives (*broiled* and *baked*) come before the nouns they describe (*chicken* and *potatoes*). But the form of *broccoli that was steamed* is different. To achieve parallelism, give the nonparallel item the same form as the others:

> **Parallel:** Dinner consisted of broiled chicken, baked potatoes, and **steamed broccoli**.
>
> > The adjective *roasted* has been placed before *chicken*.

In the above example, the parallel forms are adjective-noun combinations. When using parallelism, note the grammatical forms you are using. Match nouns with nouns, verb forms with the same types of verb forms, and so on, as in the following examples:

- **Nouns:** rain, hail, and sleet
- **Adjectives:** tall, dark, and handsome
- **Prepositional phrases:** over the moon and beyond the rainbow
- **-ing phrases that end in nouns:** singing duets, playing the piano, and dancing the tango
- **Clauses in the past tense:** he washed and she dried

12a   The uses of parallelism

When presenting a series of items

> **Not parallel:** On summer weekends, my family spends time hiking, visiting friends, and *they go to the movies*.
> **Parallel:** On summer weekends, my family spends time hiking, visiting friends, and **going to the movies**.
>
> > The sentences list a series of activities. *Hiking* and *visiting* both end in *-ing*. To be parallel, *they go to the movies* must be revised to include an *-ing* word.

For pairs of ideas linked by connecting words, such as *and* and *or*.

Other connecting words are *either . . . or, neither . . . nor*, and *not only . . . but also*.

> **Not parallel:** My older brother and *the only sister I have* are not coming to my wedding.
> **Parallel:** My older brother and **my only sister** are not coming to my wedding.
>
> > *My older brother* and *the only sister I have* are connected by the conjunction *and*, so they have equal roles in the sentence. They need to be worded in parallel form.

Not parallel: The painters were not only late but also *were messy*.
Parallel: The painters were not only late but also **messy**.

> Since the adjective *late* follows *not only*, the adjective *messy* must follow *but also*.

In comparisons using *than* or *as*. The items being compared should be presented in parallel form.

Not parallel: It is often kinder to tell a partial truth than *revealing* the whole truth.
Parallel: It is often kinder to tell a partial truth than **to reveal** the whole truth.

> In the parallel version, the two items being compared begin with *to* plus the basic form of the verb (*to tell* and *to reveal*).

12b The effects of parallelism

Parallelism will help you write more smoothly and clearly and eliminate awkward language from your papers. In general, parallelism adds power and polish to writing.

Many famous speeches and pieces of writing feature skillful parallelism. The matching form of their words and phrases helps makes them memorable.

> "I know not how others may feel, but as for me, give me liberty or give me death!"—Patrick Henry

>> Would Henry's speech have had the same ring if he'd said, ". . . give me liberty or else I would prefer to die"?

> "I have a dream that my four little children will one day live in a nation where they will not be judged by the color of their skin, but by the content of their character."—Martin Luther King, Jr.

>> Dr. King's words gain power because "by the color of their skin" and "by the content of their character" have the same form. His statement would have been much less forceful if he had said instead, ". . . not be judged by the color of their skin but by the kind of people that they are."

Also consider the following use that one student, Jon Carney, made of parallelism:

> Some of my best childhood memories are of my parents' New Year's Eve parties. Some guests came in sequins; others showed up in jeans. The spicy aromas of cold cuts and pickles mingled with the sweet scents of after-shaves and cologne.

>> Those sentences would have been less impressive had Jon written, "Some guests came in sequined outfits. Jeans were also worn to the party. Among the foods my parents served were spicy cold cuts and pickles. The sweet scents of after-shaves and cologne filled the house."

13 / Sentence Variety and Style

Writing clearly and correctly is only part of your challenge as a writer. You should also aim for variety and meaningful emphasis. As you revise, design sentences of varying lengths and patterns. Use the patterns to show the relative importance of ideas.

Following are some ways to add variety and emphasis to your writing.

13a Combine simple sentences into compound or complex sentences.

Use compound and complex sentences to emphasize or subordinate ideas and to highlight relationships. Also, use a mix of sentence types for variety.

Use coordination to create compound sentences. Give ideas equal emphasis by joining them in compound sentences (see 5b, page 7). To do so, use one of the following two methods:

1 Combine simple sentences with a comma followed by a coordinating conjunction, such as *and* or *but*.

> **Simple sentences:** It rained all morning. The sky was cloudless by noon.
> **Compound sentence:** It rained all morning, **but** the sky was cloudless by noon.

>> The simple sentences have been connected by using a comma plus the coordinating conjunction *but*. But highlights the contrast between the two ideas.

There are seven coordinating conjunctions: *and, but, so, for, yet, or,* and *nor*. In addition to connecting ideas, they clarify the relationships between clauses, as illustrated below.

> The driver failed to signal, **and** he went through a stop sign.

>> *And* shows addition: The driver's second error is added to the first one.

> I felt like sleeping, **but** I still had two hours of homework.

>> *But* shows contrast: The wish to sleep contrasts with the need to stay up and study.

> The meal was not hot, **so** we sent it back to the kitchen.

>> *So* shows the effect of a previously stated cause: The cause was the cool meal; the effect was that it was sent back to the kitchen.

> I work at home, **for** I want to be with my two young children.

>> *For* shows the cause of a previously stated effect: The cause is the desire to be with the children; the effect is that the speaker works at home.

> My brother loves cooking, **yet** he decided to major in business.

>> *Yet* shows contrast: The brother's choice of major differs from his true interest.

> You can ride with us to the game, **or** you can go in someone else's car.

>> *Or* introduces a second alternative: A second way to go to the game is added to the first one.

> Eli does not eat meat, **nor** does he eat fish.

>> *Nor* introduces a second negative statement: The point that Eli doesn't eat fish is added to the statement that he doesn't eat meat.

2 Join two closely related simple sentences with a semicolon.

> **Simple sentences:** Twenty students were registered for class. Only eight were present.
> **Compound sentence:** Twenty students were registered for class; only eight were present.

The semicolon is often followed by a transitional expression such as one of those in the box below. Like coordinating conjunctions, transitional expressions clarify the relationships between ideas.

Common Transitional Expressions

afterwards	for instance	meanwhile
also	furthermore	moreover
as a result	however	nevertheless
besides	in addition	on the other hand
consequently	in fact	otherwise
finally	in other words	then
for example	instead	therefore

> **Compound sentence:** Twenty students were registered for class; **however,** only eight were present.
>> *However* emphasizes the contrast between the two parts of this sentence.

Use subordination to create complex sentences.
Give ideas unequal emphasis by combining them into complex sentences. As a rule, put the idea you wish to emphasize in an independent clause (the clause that can stand alone as a sentence), and subordinate the less important idea or ideas by putting them in dependent clauses. (For information on the types of dependent clauses, see 4b, page 6.)

A dependent clause often begins with a subordinating conjunction or a relative pronoun. Common subordinating conjunctions and relative pronouns are in the following two boxes; each box is followed by examples.

Subordinating Conjunctions

after	because	if	unless	where
although	before	since	until	wherever
as	even if	so that	when	whether
as if	even though	though	whenever	while

> **Simple sentences:** The sun is low in the sky. A mural of tree shadows appears on the bedroom wall.
> **Complex sentence: When** the sun is low in the sky, a mural of tree shadows appears on the bedroom wall.
>> The word *when* changes an independent clause into a dependent one and clarifies the time relationship between two clauses.

Remember that when writing a complex sentence, you should generally put the idea you want to emphasize in the independent clause:

> **After** the dog barked, the doorbell rang.
>> The ringing of the doorbell is emphasized.

> **Before** the doorbell rang, the dog barked.
>> The dog's barking is emphasized.

Relative Pronouns

who	whose	whom	which	that

Relative pronoun clauses describe nouns and pronouns.

> **Simple sentences:** My guitar teacher is very patient. He plays with a local band.
> **Complex sentence:** My guitar teacher, **who plays with a local band**, is very patient.
>> The dependent clause describes the word *teacher*.

> **Simple sentences:** To the cauliflower, add some saffron. Saffron comes in tiny packets.
> **Complex sentence:** To the cauliflower, add some saffron, **which comes in tiny packets**.
>> The dependent clause describes the word *saffron*.

Punctuation note: When relative pronoun clauses provide nonessential information, as above, they are set off by commas. When they provide essential information, they are not set off by commas.

> The man **who usually sleeps by the steps of City Hall** is not there today.
>> The boldfaced clause is essential. Without it, we would not know which man is being referred to.

13b Use a variety of sentence types and elements.

Use various sentence types. Try to use a variety of sentence types in your writing. Too much of the same kind of sentence can be dull and choppy. Also, you can organize your ideas more meaningfully with differing sentence structures. For example, read this paragraph:

> There was a lack of convenient transportation at the beginning of the nineteenth century. The stagecoach was the major form of transportation. It wasn't a very comfortable one. Twelve passengers were crowded into the coach. It traveled at just four miles an hour. Roads were mostly dirt. They were usually either rutted or muddy. These were unpleasant conditions. Many people preferred to stay home.

Notice how choppy the passage is at points. It has a dull rhythm because it is made up entirely of simple sentences. Also, the relationships between ideas aren't clear. Below is a revision. Some simple sentences have been combined into compound sentences and a complex sentence, which add interest and meaning to the paragraph.

> There was a lack of convenient transportation at the beginning of the nineteenth century. The stagecoach was the major form of transportation, and it wasn't a very comfortable one. Twelve passengers were crowded into the coach, which traveled at just four miles an hour. Roads were mostly dirt, so they were usually either rutted or muddy. Because of these unpleasant conditions, many people preferred to stay home.

In addition to using simple, compound, and complex sentences of various lengths, add variety to your writing with an occasional question, command, or exclamation. (See 5a, page 7.)

What do you think is in that cubic foot of air in front of your nose? A few dust particles, you say? Guess again. That transparent square of space contains bits of skin and soil, parts of insect limbs, radio waves from outer space, fragments of dead stars, and more.

Use compound elements. A great deal of information can be communicated in one sentence by using compound elements.

> The **helpful tax** accountant was a **friendly young** man in a wheelchair.

> Pairing adjectives is one way to combine ideas that might otherwise end up in two less interesting sentences: The tax accountant was a young man in a wheelchair. He was helpful and friendly.

> **Punctuation note:** Use commas between two or more adjectives that can be joined by *and*: My husband refuses to throw away his **old, ragged** [old *and* ragged] shirt. (See 16d, page 27.)

While we waited for our waiter, he **took** a phone call, **chatted** with the cashier, and **disappeared** into the kitchen.

> One subject *(he)* has a compound verb *(took, chatted, and disappeared)*. What might have been two or three dull simple sentences are combined into one longer, more interesting one.

A mesh of white flakes blanketed the apple **blossoms**, the tomato **plants**, and a startled **robin**.

> A series of nouns provides a stream of images to suggest a late spring snow.

Use verbals (infinitives, participles, and gerunds). Verbals are words that are formed from verbs but that do not function as verbs. There are three kinds of verbals: infinitives, participles, and gerunds. Use them to add variety to your writing.

The infinitive. The infinitive is formed by adding the base form of the verb to the word *to*, as in *to go* or *to work*. An infinitive generally describes or explains other words in the sentence. (It may also function as a noun.) To add variety to your writing, try beginning some sentences with infinitives. An infinitive or an infinitive phrase that begins a sentence is usually followed by a comma.

> **To knit**, all you need are needles, yarn, and patience.

> **To reach a goal**, you usually must aim for it.

The participle. Present participles end in *-ing*. Most past participles end in *-ed*. This type of verbal always functions as an adjective. Sometimes a participle comes before the word being described.

> The **snoring** man never heard the burglar enter his home.

> The **painted** desk was bought at a garage sale.

Participles and participial phrases can be used effectively at the beginning of sentences. In that position, they must be followed by the word they describe:

> **Delayed**, Marge came home too late to see her son's Little League game.

> **Being creative**, I thought of a good reason to put off doing my homework.

Participles and participial phrases can also be effectively used within sentences after the words they describe:

> An old couch, **sagging deeply**, sat on the curb.

> The cake, **decorated to look like a Social Security card**, was for someone's sixty-fifth birthday.

> **Punctuation note:** In general, when a participial phrase begins a sentence, follow it with a comma. When a participial phrase comes in the middle of a sentence, interrupting the flow of the sentence, place commas before and after the phrase.

The gerund. A gerund is an *-ing* word (in the form of a present participle) that is used as a noun.

> There is no reason for your **lying**.

> **Agreeing with Susan** is often easier than **arguing with her**.

Use prepositional phrases and adverbs to begin sentences. Another way to achieve variety is by beginning sentences with prepositional phrases and adverbs.

Prepositional phrases. A prepositional phrase begins with a preposition and ends with a noun, the object of the preposition. Common prepositions include *in, on, of, by, from, across, before, under*, and *behind*. (See page 3 for a longer list of prepositions.) When the prepositional phrase comes at the beginning of the sentence, it is generally followed by a comma.

> **In the dark basement,** I heard breathing.

Prepositional phrases are generally found within a sentence. As a result, beginning a sentence with one draws attention to a description of time, place, or the like. It also allows the writer to place a more dramatic idea at the end, as in the second sentence below.

> **Preposition within a sentence:** I began sneezing uncontrollably **during the love scene**.
> **Preposition at the beginning: During the love scene**, I began sneezing uncontrollably.

Adverbs ending in -*ly*. When an adverb ending in *-ly* is at the beginning of a sentence, it is usually followed by a comma.

> **Expertly,** Cliff changed the baby's diaper.

> **Selfishly,** I ate both deliciously chewy ends of the fresh rye bread.

Adverbs ending in *-ly* may be used in more than one place within a sentence. The first sentence above, for example, might be written as follows: Cliff changed the baby's diaper *expertly*. Beginning with an *-ly* word generally draws attention to how something is done.

Use appositives. An **appositive** is a word or phrase that renames, or identifies, a noun or pronoun. The appositive follows the word or words it explains.

> The only air conditioning in Ed's car, **a twelve-year-old Volkswagen bug**, was a hole in the floor.

Turning a simple sentence into an appositive is one way to combine two sentences into one more interesting sentence.

Two sentences: Greta Garbo retired from filmmaking at the age of thirty-six. She was a beautiful and adored actress.

One sentence: Greta Garbo, **a beautiful and adored actress**, retired from filmmaking at the age of thirty-six.

> **Punctuation note:** When an appositive is not essential to the main meaning of a sentence, it is set off by commas, as above. Most appositives are not essential to the meaning of a sentence. They may add interesting information, but the sentence makes full sense without them. Without its appositive, for example, the sentence above still makes sense: Greta Garbo retired from filmmaking at the age of thirty-six.

14 / Word Choice

A sentence may be grammatically correct, yet fail to communicate well because of the words that the writer has chosen. This section explains common types of ineffective word choice: slang, jargon, clichés, wordiness, showy language, and sexist language.

14a Slang

Slang expressions are lively and fun to use, but they should be avoided in formal writing. One problem with slang is that it's not always understood by all readers. Slang used by members of a particular group (such as teenagers or science-fiction fans) may be unfamiliar to people outside the group. Also, slang tends to change rapidly. What was *cool* for one generation is *awesome* for another. Finally, slang is by nature informal. So while it adds color to our everyday speech, it is generally out of place in writing for school or work. Use slang only when you have a specific purpose in mind, such as being humorous or communicating the flavor of an informal conversation.

Slang: After a *bummer of a* movie, we *pigged out on* a pizza.
Revision: After a **disappointing** movie, we **devoured** a pizza.

14b Jargon

Jargon is the specialized language of a particular field, such as any of the various types of professional, business, and entertainment fields. For instance, a lawyer's language includes such specialized terms as *magistrate*, *tort*, and *writ*. Avoid using unexplained jargon for an audience that will be unfamiliar with it.

Jargon: Many myocardial infarctions result from atherosclerosis.
Revision: Many **heart attacks** result from **a form of hardening of the arteries**.

14c Clichés

A **cliché** is an expression that was once lively and colorful. However, because it has been used too often, it has become dull and boring. Try to use fresh wording in place of predictable expressions. Following are a few of the clichés to avoid in your writing:

Common Clichés

avoid like the plague	pie in the sky
better late than never	pretty as a picture
bored to tears	sad but true
easy as pie	sick and tired
in the nick of time	sigh of relief
in this day and age	time and time again
last but not least	tried and true
light as a feather	under the weather
make ends meet	without a doubt

Cliché: My new advisor is *as sharp as a tack*.
Revision: My new advisor is **very insightful**.

14d Wordiness

Some writers think that using more words than necessary makes their writing sound important. Actually, wordiness just annoys and confuses your reader. Try to edit your writing carefully. First of all, remove words that mean the same as other words in the sentence.

Wordy: Though *huge in size* and *blood red in color*, the cartoon monster had a sweet personality.
Revision: Though **huge** and **blood red**, the cartoon monster had a sweet personality.

> *Huge* refers to size, so the words *in size* can be removed with no loss of meaning. *Red* is a color, so the words *in color* are also unnecessary.

Wordy: I finally *made up my mind and decided* to look for a new job.
Revision: I finally **decided** to look for a new job.

Note how the wordy expressions below can be made concise by eliminating repetitive words.

Examples of Wordiness Due to Repetition

few ~~in number~~	green ~~in color~~
postponed ~~until later~~	small ~~in size~~
~~hurriedly~~ rushed	punched ~~with his fist~~
listened ~~with her ears~~	~~the feeling of~~ sadness
the first paragraph ~~at the beginning~~ of the chapter	

Secondly, avoid puffed-up phrases that can be expressed in a word or two instead.

Wordy: *Due to the fact that* the printer was out of paper, Renee went to a store *for the purpose of buying more*.
Revision: **Because** the printer was out of paper, Renee went to a store **to buy more**.

Notice how easily each of the wordy expressions on the next page can be replaced by one word:

Wordy Expression	Concise Replacement
a large number of	many
at an earlier point in time	before
at this point in time	now
be in possession of	have
due to the fact that	because
during the time that	while
each and every day	daily
in order to	to
in the event that	if
in the near future	soon
in this day and age	today
made the decision to	decided

In general, work to express your thoughts in the fewest words possible that are still complete and clear. Because writers initially concentrate on ideas and organization, early drafts are often wordy. When revising, watch for repetition that can be eliminated and wordy expressions that can be replaced, as well as other opportunities to eliminate wordiness. For example, sentences with such beginnings as *there was* or *it is* can often be condensed.

Wordy: *There was* a mountain lion *that was* roaming the suburbs.
Revision: A mountain lion was roaming the suburbs.

Phrases and clauses can often be shortened.

Wordy: *A number of* studies of people who experienced *the event of* a major earthquake reveal some *of the* psychological effects *that natural disasters can have on people.*
Revision: Studies of people who experienced a major earthquake reveal some psychological effects of natural disasters.

Words can sometimes be eliminated by combining sentences.

Wordy: The Civilian Conservation Corps was established in 1933. *It was created* to provide jobs during the Depression.
Revision: The Civilian Conservation Corps was established in 1933 to provide jobs during the Depression.

14e Showy language

While it is very useful to expand your vocabulary, avoid using long words and sentences just to impress. A flowery, overblown style calls attention to the words themselves at the expense of the ideas.

Showy: Please place the *refuse receptacles* by the *sidewalk-street boundary.*
Revision: Please put the **trash cans** by the **curb**.

14f Sexist language

Sexist language characterizes people or roles solely according to gender. To avoid sexist language, do not refer to people in general as *men* or *mankind;* instead use a term such as *people* or *humankind.* Instead of *manpower,* use a term such as *human resources.* Also, do not refer to an unknown individual as *he.* Instead, use *he or she,* or recast the sentence so you can use the plural *they.*

Sexist: The average American saves too little of *his* income each year.
Revision: The average American saves too little of **his or her** income each year.
Revision: Average **Americans** save too little of **their** income**s** each year.

Also, avoid describing or identifying men and women in different ways. For instance, don't describe women by their clothes or their marital status if you are not doing the same for men.

Sexist: Co-chairing the art auction are Julius Brown, first vice-president of Neighborhood Banks, Inc., and *Mrs.* Freda Wright, *wife of Dr. Ellis Wright.*
Revision: Co-chairing the art auction are Julius Brown, first vice-president of Neighborhood Banks, Inc., and Freda Wright, **art teacher at South High School**.

You can also avoid sexist language by using gender-neutral words for jobs and other roles when both sexes may be included. For example, don't assume that a nurse is necessarily *she* and that a doctor is necessarily *he.* Don't refer to an individual as a *female engineer* or a *male kindergarten teacher,* which may imply that women are inferior engineers and that men are poor kindergarten teachers.

Sexist: A politician must spend much of *his* time running for office.
Revision: A politician must spend much of **his or her** time running for office.
Revision: **Politicians** must spend much of **their** time running for office.

Following are some titles commonly considered sexist, along with corresponding nonsexist terms:

Sexist Position Titles	Alternatives
businessman	businessperson
chairman	chairperson, chair
congressman	congressperson
fireman	firefighter
mailman	letter carrier, mail carrier
policeman	police officer
sculptress	sculptor
stewardess	flight attendant

15 / End Marks

15a The period .

Use a period at the end of a statement, a mild command, or an indirect question.

The children jumped over all the rain puddles.

Hand me the red pen.

I wonder if there will be a surprise quiz today.

Use a period after many abbreviations. Common abbreviations with periods include the following:

Mr.	B.A.	B.C.
Ms.	R.N.	etc.
Mrs.	M.D.	a.m. (or A.M.)

A period is not used in abbreviations of names of organizations and government agencies (such as NBC and the IRS) and in U.S. Postal Service abbreviations for states (such as FL, IL, and TX).

15b The question mark ?

Use a question mark after a sentence that asks a direct question.

Are you ready for the exam?

"Can I have your phone number?" Lynda asked Phil.

Some writers prefer not to use a question mark after a polite request worded as a question.

Would you please forward this letter.

Do not put a question mark

- At the end of an indirect question. **Indirect questions** tell the reader about questions, rather than asking them directly. They end with periods, not question marks.

  Incorrect: The instructor asked if we were ready for the exam?
  Correct: The instructor asked if we were ready for the exam.

  Incorrect: Lynda asked Phil if she could have his phone number?
  Correct: Lynda asked Phil if she could have his phone number.

15c The exclamation point !

Use an exclamation point after a word or statement that expresses extreme emotion or surprise or that gives a strong command.

Wow!

Help! Somebody help me!

Note: Exclamation points lose their power if they are used too frequently. By choosing your words carefully, you can often show strong feeling without an exclamation point, as in this sentence: The cat was stretched out limply in the middle of the road, lifeless.

16 / The Comma ,

A comma often indicates a slight pause. It is used to separate parts of a sentence.

Use a comma as follows:

16a Between independent clauses connected by a coordinating conjunction (*and, but, so, or, nor, for,* or *yet*)

Put a comma before (*not* after) a coordinating conjunction that connects two or more independent clauses into one sentence. An independent clause is a word group that can stand alone as a separate sentence.

Gabe eats like a horse, **but** he is pencil-thin.

Exception: If the two independent clauses are short, the comma may be omitted, especially before *and* or *or*: You jog and I'll walk.

Do not put a comma

- Between two equal parts of a sentence that are not independent clauses.

  Incorrect: My neighbor's dog dislikes children, and hates the mailman.
  Correct: My neighbor's dog dislikes children and hates the mailman.

- Between independent clauses that have no coordinating conjunction between them. (See 10b, page 19.)

  Incorrect: Matt is a great pitcher, he is a great dancer too.
  Correct: Matt is a great pitcher. He is a great dancer too.

16b After introductory material

Use a comma to separate introductory phrases and clauses from the rest of the sentence.

After a hot shower, Vince fell asleep on the sofa.

To reach me tomorrow, you'll have to call my car phone.

As the movie credits rolled, we stretched and headed toward the exits.

Exception: Short introductory material need not be followed by a comma as long as the meaning is clear: While driving I listen to self-help tapes.

16c Between items in a series

The comma is used to separate items in a series of three or more.

School cafeterias have learned not to serve **broccoli, spinach,** or **Brussels sprouts**.

Our tasks for the party include **blowing up balloons, setting the table,** and **planning the music**.

I wrote out my résumé, my mother corrected it, and **my brother typed it**.

Do not use a comma or commas

- When using *and* or *or* between all the items in the series.

  Incorrect: School cafeterias have learned not to serve broccoli, *or* spinach, *or* Brussels sprouts.

Correct: School cafeterias have learned not to serve broccoli **or** spinach **or** Brussels sprouts.

- When a list contains only two items.

    Incorrect: School cafeterias have learned not to serve spinach, or Brussels sprouts.

    Correct: School cafeterias have learned not to serve spinach **or** Brussels sprouts.

16d Between coordinate adjectives

Put a comma between **coordinate adjectives**—adjectives that sound right when joined with *and*. Such adjectives each modify the noun separately.

Cecelia has a **cheerful, friendly** smile.

Cheerful and friendly smile sounds right.

The tomb contained a **large gold** mask.

Large and gold mask does not sound right.

16e To set off transitional and other parenthetical expressions and absolute phrases

A word or word group that interrupts the flow of thought in a sentence should be set off by commas.

Transitional and other parenthetical expressions.
Transitional expressions are words or word groups that help connect ideas and sentences. They include such words and phrases as *however, furthermore, as a result,* and *on the other hand.* (A list of transitional words is on page 29.) Parenthetical expressions should generally be set off with commas.

Of course, it started to rain after I'd watered my garden.

I had also, **believe it or not,** just washed my car.

Notes: (1) Commas may be omitted around certain short transitional expressions if you feel they do not interrupt the flow of thought: I therefore went to sleep early. (2) Transitional words may be used after a semicolon to connect two independent clauses. To see how to punctuate in such cases, see 17b, pages 28–29.

Absolute phrases. Absolute phrases modify the whole sentence, not just a part of it. (See 3c, page 6.) They should be set off with commas.

His tail wagging, our dog barked halfheartedly at the mail carrier.

Lanelle, **her voice trembling,** explained what had happened.

16f Around nonessential clauses and phrases (including appositives)

Note: Grammar books often refer to nonessential elements as "nonrestrictive elements" and to essential descriptions as "restrictive elements."

Nonessential clauses and phrases. A nonessential clause provides a description that is not essential to the meaning of the sentence. The description may be interesting, but the word being described is clear without it.

Such clauses are interrupters and should be set off with commas.

To find out whether a clause is nonessential, try reading the sentence without it. If the word being described is clear without it, then the clause is nonessential.

Nonessential: Harvey, **who came to the party with Joy,** says he was kidnapped by aliens.

If the boldfaced clause were removed, we would still know who said he was kidnapped by aliens: Harvey says he was kidnapped by aliens.

However, a clause that is needed to identify another word in the sentence is not an interrupter. Since it answers the question "Which one?" (or "Which ones?"), it is essential and should not be set off with commas.

Essential: The man **who came to the party with Joy** says he was kidnapped by aliens.

Without the boldfaced words, we would *not* know who said he was kidnapped by aliens: The man says he was kidnapped by aliens. (Which man?)

Hint: If the word *who, whom,* or *which* can be replaced by *that,* then you know the clause is essential. "Harvey **that came to the party** . . ." does not sound right. "A man **that came to the party** . . ." does.

As with descriptive clauses, descriptive phrases should be set off by commas if they are nonessential. Phrases that are essential should not be set off with commas.

Nonessential: The mayor's house, **with a red front door and shutters,** is easy to find.
Essential: The house **with a red front door and shutters** belongs to the mayor.

Nonessential appositives. An **appositive** is a word or word group that renames a noun or pronoun. Nonessential appositives are set off by commas. Essential appositives are not.

Nonessential: "The Star-Spangled Banner," **the American national anthem,** was written to the melody of an eighteenth-century drinking song.

This sentence would be clear without the appositive: "The Star-Spangled Banner" was written to the melody of an eighteenth-century drinking song.

Essential: Robert Louis Stevenson dreamed the plot of his novel ***The Strange Case of Dr. Jekyll and Mr. Hyde***.

Since Stevenson wrote more than one novel, this sentence would not be clear without the appositive: Robert Louis Stevenson dreamed the plot of his novel. (Which novel?)

16g To set off words of direct address, *yes* and *no*, mild interjections, expressions of contrast, and tag questions

Words of direct address. Use commas to set off names or other words used to address directly the person or people being spoken to.

You, **Mr. Gimble,** are the lucky winner of a ballpoint pen.

Yes and *no*. Use commas to set off *yes* and *no* at the beginning of a sentence.

> **No,** you cannot have a raise.

Mild interjections. Use commas to set off words such as *well, ah*, and *oh*.

> **Well,** that's a shame.

> **Note:** Follow an interjection that represents strong emotion with an exclamation point: Wow! I won.

Expressions of contrast. Sharply contrasting elements that begin with such words as *not, but*, and *unlike* should be set off with commas.

> The American flag was designed by Francis Hopkinson, **not** Betsy Ross.

Tag questions. Set off added-on questions with a comma, and end the sentence with a question mark.

> We were certainly lucky the storm passed us by, **weren't we**?

16h To set off direct quotations

Use commas to separate direct quotations from such words as *he wrote* or *she said*.

> "Children," wrote a wise man, "need models rather than critics."

> **Exception:** When quoted words are blended into a sentence, they are not set off by a comma. The word *that* often precedes quoted words that are blended into a sentence: Mark Twain wrote **that** some people think public opinion "is the voice of God."

> **Note:** Do not use a comma to set off an indirect quotation, which reports on what was said instead of exactly quoting it.

> > **Incorrect:** A wise man wrote that, children need models, not critics.
> > **Correct:** A wise man wrote that children need models, not critics.

16i With dates, addresses, letters, and titles

Use commas with dates, addresses, letters, and titles according to established usage. (For the use of the comma in numerals, see 25d, page 38.)

Within a date. Place commas after the the day of the week (if used), the date, and the year.

> Professor Ruiz is getting married on **Friday, December 27, 1996**.

> **Exception:** If only the month and year are given, no comma is used: Our lease runs from May 1996 through April 1998.

In an address within a sentence. Place a comma after each part of the address *except* between the state and the ZIP code.

> Send your comments about this book to **Townsend Press, Pavilions at Greentree, Suite 408, Marlton, NJ 08053**.

In informal letters. Place a comma after the opening and closing.

> Dear Grandma, . . . With love,

> **Note:** In business letters, a colon is used after the opening: Dear Mr. Cramer**:**

With titles. When a person's name is followed by an abbreviated title (including a degree), set off the title with commas.

> ◆Martin Luther King, **Jr.,** inspired a generation of civil-rights workers.

16j To prevent misreading

Use a comma to separate words that might otherwise be misread.

> **Incorrect:** Before the movie cheered us up.
> **Correct:** Before**,** the movie cheered us up.

16k Misuses of the comma

In general, use a comma only when a comma rule applies or when a comma is otherwise needed to help a sentence read clearly. Do not use a comma in the following situations:

Between a subject and its verb

> **Incorrect:** The rubber band, was invented in the mid-1800s.
> **Correct:** The rubber band was invented in the mid-1800s.

Between a verb and its object

> **Incorrect:** Irving Berlin played, the piano.
> **Correct:** Irving Berlin played the piano.

17 / The Semicolon   ;

A semicolon can be used to join independent clauses. It is also used between items in a series when the items themselves contain commas.
Use a semicolon as follows:

17a To join two independent clauses that are closely related but are not connected by a coordinating conjunction (such as *and, but*, or *so*)

> The cat knocked over a can of cola**;** the soda foamed over the white carpet.

> > The two independent clauses could have been separated by a period. However, the author has stressed their close relationship by using a semicolon instead.

17b To join two closely related independent clauses with a transitional word or phrase

The transitional word or phrase shows the relationship between the two independent clauses. When it comes right after the semicolon, it is usually followed with a comma. (See also 10c, Method 4, page 19.)

Common Transitional Expressions

afterwards	for instance	meanwhile
also	furthermore	moreover
as a result	however	nevertheless
besides	in addition	on the other hand
consequently	in fact	otherwise
finally	in other words	then
for example	instead	therefore

> Marta began school without knowing any English; nevertheless, she will graduate at the top of her class.

> The transitional word *nevertheless* clarifies the contrast between the two independent clauses.

17c To separate items in a series when the items themselves contain commas

Items in a series are usually separated by commas. However, if the items already contain commas, prevent confusion by using semicolons to separate the items.

> Driving down Sunset Strip, we passed La Boutique, which sells women's clothing; The Friendly Cafe, which serves twenty different kinds of coffee; and Pet Palace, which sells snakes, parrots, and spiders.

17d Misuses of the semicolon

Do not use a semicolon in the following situations:

Between an introductory phrase and the rest of the sentence

Incorrect: His hands trembling; the speaker admitted that he was nervous.
Correct: His hands trembling, the speaker admitted that he was nervous.

Between a dependent clause and an independent clause

Incorrect: Although the garbage collectors have no contract; they have agreed to continue working.
Correct: Although the garbage collectors have no contract, they have agreed to continue working.

To introduce a list

Incorrect: The suitcase was filled with everything but clothing; books, games, snacks, crayons, and a teddy bear.
Correct: The suitcase was filled with everything but clothing: books, games, snacks, crayons, and a teddy bear.

18 / The Colon :

The colon comes at the end of an independent clause to direct attention to what follows. It is also used to separate parts of conventional material.

Use a colon as follows:

18a To direct attention to what follows

A list. A colon may be used to introduce a list that follows an independent clause. The clause may include words such as *the following* or *as follows.*

> On her first day of vacation, Carrie did three things: she watched a funny movie, took a long nap, and ate at her favorite restaurant.

> Students must bring the following items to the drawing class: a sketch pad, a charcoal pencil, and a rubber eraser.

An appositive. After an independent clause, a colon can be used to introduce an **appositive**—a word or words that rename or identify a nearby noun or pronoun.

> Frederic Dannay and Manfred B. Lee wrote under one pen name: Ellery Queen.

A quotation. A quotation can be introduced by an independent clause followed by a colon.

> Eleanor Roosevelt wrote this about courage: "You gain strength, courage and confidence by every experience in which you really stop to look fear in the face. You are able to say to yourself, 'I lived through this horror. I can take the next thing that comes along.'"

A second independent clause that explains or illustrates the first one

> Bert suddenly cancelled his evening plans for a simple reason: his [*or* His] car was out of gas.

A business letter. Put a colon after the greeting of a business letter.

> Dear Sir or Madam:

> **Note:** Use a comma after the greeting of a personal letter: Dear Mom,

18b To separate parts of conventional material

Hours and minutes. 3:15 p.m.

Title and subtitle. *I Had a Hammer: The Hank Aaron Story*

Biblical chapter and verse references. Matthew 7:7

> **Note:** The Modern Language Association guidelines call for a period: Matthew 7.7

In bibliographic entries

> **Place of publication and the publisher.** Boston: Houghton Mifflin

> **Volume number and page numbers.** *Smithsonian* 25: 90–99

18c Misuses of the colon

Do not use a colon in the following situations:

Between a verb and its object

> **Incorrect:** Roxanne collects: stamps, coins, and husbands.
> **Correct:** Roxanne collects stamps, coins, and husbands.

Between a verb and the subject complement

> **Incorrect:** The dog's name is: Stuart.
> **Correct:** The dog's name is Stuart.

Between a preposition and its object

Incorrect: Jean lives with: two cats, a dog, and a six-foot python.
Correct: Jean lives with two cats, a dog, and a six-foot python.

After *including, for example,* or *such as*

Incorrect: Geese have become a nuisance at such places as: yards, roads, and golf courses.
Correct: Geese have become a nuisance at such places as yards, roads, and golf courses.

19 / The Apostrophe '

The apostrophe is used to show possession. It is also used in contractions and certain plurals.

Use an apostrophe as follows:

19a To show possession

Possessives show ownership, or belonging. Possession can be expressed in a phrase that contains the word *of*. For example, *the waiting room of the doctor* means the same as *the doctor's waiting room*. If you're not sure if a word is possessive, try turning it into a phrase with *of*.

Following are ways to change the form of nouns and indefinite pronouns to show possession.

Adding an apostrophe plus s. Add *-'s* to form the possessives of the following:

- **All singular nouns**, including those that end in *s*

  The coat's lining is torn.

  The press's right to print unpopular views is protected by the First Amendment.

  Note: When adding *-'s* makes a word hard to pronounce, many writers omit the *s*: Norman Cousins' experiences with illness taught him that laughter can improve one's health.

- **Plural nouns that do not end in s**

  Holly often buys clothes from the men's department.

- **Indefinite pronouns** (pronouns, such as *nobody* and *everyone*, which do not refer to a specific person or thing)

  Someone's dog was barking all night.

Adding only an apostrophe. To form the possessive of plural nouns that end in *s*, add only an apostrophe.

The Clarks' family tree goes back two hundred years.

We're going to the Joneses' house for dinner tonight.

Joint and individual possession. To show joint possession by two or more nouns, add an apostrophe to only the last noun.

Beth and Jeremy's new van broke down on the highway.

If each noun possesses something individually, each one gets an apostrophe.

Boys' and girls' shoes are sized differently.

Hyphenated words. To show possession in a hyphenated noun, add the apostrophe to the last part of the word.

Mr. Wright has been working part-time at his brother-in-law's pizza place.

19b To mark omissions in contractions

The apostrophe takes the place of missing letters in contractions.

I can't [cannot] believe that you're [you are] really in town.

The apostrophe also takes the place of the missing first two numerals in years.

The computer has greatly changed our lives in the '90s [1990s].

19c To form the plurals of letters, abbreviations, words referred to as words, and numerals

Kenneth received two *B*'s and two *C*'s this semester.

There are numerous YMCA's throughout the country.

The parents of a two-year-old hear many *no*'s throughout a day.

The address is easy to remember—it has four 7's in a row.

Note: The plural of decades can be shown either with or without an apostrophe: In the 1930's [*or* 1930s], an inventor named Earl D. Tupper experimented with a strong new plastic.

19d Misuses of the apostrophe

An apostrophe should not be used in the following situations:

In plurals that are not possessives. A plural that is not possessive is formed simply by adding *-s* or *-es* to a noun.

Incorrect: The daffodil's are peeking through the snow.
Correct: The **daffodils** are peeking through the snow.

In verbs. Many verbs end with an *s*. Do not use an apostrophe in a verb.

Incorrect: Jenny play's poker once a week.
Correct: Jenny **plays** poker once a week.

In possessive pronouns. There is no apostrophe in the possessive pronouns *his, hers, its, ours, yours, theirs,* and *whose*.

Incorrect: Our old tree is losing it's leaves.
Correct: Our old tree is losing **its** leaves.

Note: Do not confuse some of the possessive pronouns with contractions that look and sound similar to them.

Possessive pronouns	Contractions
your	you're (meaning *you are*)
its	it's (meaning *it is* or *it has*)
their	they're (meaning *they are*)
whose	who's (meaning *who is* or *who has*)

20 / Quotation Marks " "

Quotation marks are used to enclose the exact words of a speaker or writer as well as certain titles or words used with a special meaning.

Use quotation marks as follows:

20a   To enclose direct quotations

Put quotation marks around a direct quotation, the exact words of a speaker or writer.

> "Your car is in big trouble," the mechanic muttered to Fred.

> "We cannot solve a problem by hoping that someone else will solve it for us," wrote psychiatrist M. Scott Peck.

Exception: Long quotations are indented and not enclosed within quotation marks. (For more details on indenting quotations, see 37a, page 59, and 38a, page 65.)

Quotations with split sentences. If a directly quoted sentence is split up, each part must be enclosed by a set of quotation marks.

> "After inserting the disk," said the instructor, "turn on the computer."
>
> The words *said the instructor* are not enclosed in quotation marks because they were not spoken by the instructor. The words *turn on the computer* begin with a small letter because they are a continuation of a sentence, not a new sentence. (The full sentence spoken by the instructor is "After inserting the disk, turn on the computer.")

Quotations of more than one sentence. If an uninterrupted direct quotation is more than one sentence, enclose the entire quotation in one set of quotation marks.

> Our minister always says, "It's every citizen's responsibility to vote. If you don't vote, you shouldn't complain."

If a quotation is interrupted between sentences, enclose each part of the quotation in quotation marks.

> "I really hate my job," Stan told his wife. "I think I'd better start looking for a new one."
>
> The words *Stan told his wife* are not part of the direct quotation.

Dialogue. In dialogue, which is directly quoted conversation between two or more people, start a new paragraph for each change of speaker.

> "Can I help you?" asked the waitress.
> "Just a tall cup of coffee," Ramon answered.

Quotations within quotations. Use single quotation marks (' ') to set off quotations within quotations. (On most keyboards and typewriters, use the apostrophe key to create a single quotation mark.)

> Verna said, "It was Rick who yelled 'Bravo!' during the applause."

Do not use quotation marks

- Around indirect quotations. We often express someone's spoken or written thoughts in our own words. Such statements are called **indirect quotations**. Indirect quotations should *not* be enclosed in quotation marks. (Indirect quotations often include the word *that*.)

  Incorrect: The mechanic said "that Fred's car has real problems."
  Correct: The mechanic said that Fred's car has real problems.

  Incorrect: M. Scott Peck wrote that "we cannot expect others to solve a problem for us."
  Correct: M. Scott Peck wrote that we cannot expect others to solve a problem for us.

20b   To enclose titles of short works

Put quotation marks around the titles of short stories, newspaper or magazine articles, songs, poems, episodes of TV series, book chapters, and other parts of longer works.

> Our instructor assigned the short story "The Open Boat" by Stephen Crane.

> The magazine article titled "Policing the Police" is about good cops who go bad.

Use italics, or underlining, to present titles of longer works. See 24a, page 37.

20c   To enclose words used in a special sense

Words used ironically or in another special way may be enclosed in quotation marks. Use quotation marks for this purpose sparingly.

> The "fast-food" order took twenty minutes.

Do not use quotation marks

- To enclose familiar slang.

  Incorrect: When I have to give a speech in class, I feel "uptight" for days.
  Correct: When I have to give a speech in class, I feel uptight for days.

  > Slang generally should be avoided in formal writing. (For more about slang, see 14a, page 24.)

- To show humorous intent.

  Incorrect: Dan really "fell" for his wife—he met her on the ice rink after toppling into her.

  Correct: Dan really fell for his wife—he met her on the ice rink after toppling into her.

  > Humor is generally more effective if readers are left to see it on their own.

20d   To enclose definitions

> The word *crystal* comes from a Greek word that means "ice."

20e   With other punctuation

Following are accepted ways of using quotation marks with other punctuation:

Commas. When a quotation is introduced with explanatory words such as *he said,* separate those words from the quotation with a comma. When the explanatory words come first, put the comma *before* the first quotation mark.

> My brother yelled**,** "Is *roommate* spelled with one or two *m*'s?"

When the explanatory words come after the quotation, put the comma *inside* the closing quotation mark.

> "My greatest challenge is balancing my personal life with my career**,**" Tama informed us.

> **Note:** When there are no explanatory words (like *he said*) just before the quotation and the quotation is blended into a sentence, no comma should be used: Author Bertrand Russell once referred to becoming drunk as "temporary suicide."

Periods. Put a period inside quotation marks when the sentence ends with quoted material.

> Franklin D. Roosevelt said, "Peace, like charity, begins at home**."**

> In 1877, a sixteen-year-old girl wrote the piano exercise "Chopsticks**."**

Colons and semicolons. Put colons and semicolons outside the quotation marks.

> The security guard said, "No one is allowed in here. You'll have to leave"**;** then he walked us to the door.

> There's a famous line in Alexander Pope's poem "An Essay on Criticism"**:** "A little learning is a dangerous thing."

Question marks and exclamation points. When a question mark or exclamation point applies only to the quoted words, put it within the quotation marks.

> "Where are my red shoes**?**" asked Lana.
>> The question is within the quotation marks.

> My father shouted, "Turn down that music**!**"
>> The entire exclamation is within quotation marks.

When the question mark or exclamation point applies to the whole sentence, put it *outside* the quotation marks.

> Did you say "Thank you"**?**
>> The whole sentence is the question.

> Rani's two-year-old daughter knows every word of "God Bless America"**!**
>> The emotional point is made by the entire sentence, not just by the words within quotation marks.

20f Misuses of quotation marks

Do not use quotation marks in the following situations:

Simply to emphasize one or more words

> **Incorrect:** "Promotion" of a product can take many forms.
> **Correct:** Promotion of a product can take many forms.

Around titles introducing your own papers

> **Incorrect:** "Types of Advertisements"
> **Correct:** Types of Advertisements

21 / Other Punctuation Marks

21a The hyphen   -

Hyphens are used within a word or between two words. Use a hyphen as follows:

To divide a word at the end of a line of writing. If all of a word won't fit at the end of a line, follow these guidelines:

1. Never divide a word which has only one syllable.
2. Divide words only between syllables.
3. Never divide a word in a way that leaves only one or two letters alone on a line.
4. When dividing a word that already contains a hyphen, divide where the hyphen is.

> The lawyer stood up, shoved some papers into her brief-case, and hurried to court.

To join two or more words that act as a single modifier before a noun

> The sports car swerved around the slow-moving truck.
>> *Slow* and *moving* work together to modify the noun *truck*.

> **Exceptions:**
> • Do not use a hyphen when the two words come *after* the word they modify: The truck was **slow moving**.
> • Do not use a hyphen when the first word is an *-ly* adverb: The sports car swerved around the **slowly moving** truck.

> **Note:** In a series, use the word after the hyphen only once—following the last hyphen.
>> This neighborhood has a mixture of one-, two-, and three-**story** houses.

In numbers. Hyphenate any two-word number from twenty-one to ninety-nine and any two-word fraction.

> Karen is twenty-two, and her husband is forty-two.

> Give me only a fourth of that chocolate bar; you may have the other three-fourths.

In some compound words. Compound words are made up of two or more words. Some are joined with a hyphen, such as *old-timer* and *half-hour*. Others may be written as one word (*catlike* and *redhead*) or as two words (*blue jay* and *figure skating*).

> Bonita makes extra **pocket money** by **baby-sitting**, and she does her **homework** at the same time.

There is no clear rule to cover all compound words, so when you're unsure about whether or not to hyphenate such words, check your dictionary. If a compound word is not in the dictionary, write it as two words (unless another rule calls for a hyphen).

With the prefixes *all-, self-, ex-* (when it means *former*) and the suffix *-elect*

> all-around   ex-president
> self-image   governor-elect

21b The dash   —

While the hyphen is used within or between individual words, the dash is used between parts of a sentence.

When typing, form a dash with two hyphens (--), leaving no space before, between, or after them. A dash is used for dramatic effect or for clarity; do not use it for ordinary pauses in place of a comma, period, or semicolon. Do use it for the following purposes:

To set off parenthetical material for emphasis or clarity. Use dashes to set off parenthetical material (added information, explanations, and comments that are not essential to the main point) that you wish to emphasize or that itself contains commas.

> Everyone in that family—including a teenager—has a cholesterol problem.

> The Peterson triplets—Peter, Paul, and Perry—are all on the school baseball team.

To signal the end of a list. Use a dash between an introductory list and the explanation that follows.

> Family support, prayer, and hope—these are what got Grady through all those months in jail.

To introduce a final dramatic element. Use a dash to emphasize a final explanation, list, or added point.

> Ravi hurriedly left work in the middle of the day—his wife was having labor pains.

> Anne's refrigerator was packed with food for the party—trays of cold cuts, bottles of pickles, loaves of bread, and several pitchers of lemonade.

> My wallet was found in a trash can—minus its cash.

Note: The colon can also be used to introduce some final elements. However, a colon is more formal and less dramatic than a dash.

21c Parentheses ( )

There are two common uses of parentheses:

To enclose interrupting material. Use parentheses for secondary information you wish to de-emphasize, such as minor additions and comments. When a comma, semicolon, or period immediately follows parenthetical material, put the punctuation mark after the closing parenthesis.

> According to Dr. Ford (my dentist), the mercury in fillings poses no health problem.

Note: Too many parentheses can be distracting to readers. Use commas to enclose most interrupting material.

Around numbers or letters that list items within a sentence

> Ron's work for the evening is as follows: (1) finish a history term paper, (2) read a chapter in the psychology text, and (3) wash a load of laundry.

21d Brackets [ ]

Use brackets within quoted material for the following purposes:

To enclose a clarifying word or phrase inserted into a direct quotation

> "The increased demand [for recycled trash] is due partly to an improving economy."

The words *for recycled trash* are not part of the direct quotation. The author has inserted them to make the point clear to readers.

To enclose the Latin word *sic* to show that an error was made by the original writer. *Sic* means *thus*, or *so*, and indicates that an error was made by the person being quoted.

> Mr. Elwood wrote, "I would of [sic] written sooner, but I have been ill these past weeks."

> The bracketed *sic* shows that it was Mr. Elwood who wrote *would of* instead of *would have*.

To enclose a parenthetical item within parentheses

> Mobiles (first created by artist Alexander Calder [1898–1976]) are commercially available in various sizes and materials.

21e The ellipsis   . . .

Use an ellipsis to show that words within a sentence in a quoted passage have been omitted.

> Jackson writes that in December 1918 Ripley "strung together a collage of sports oddities . . . and submitted it to his editor with the title *Champs and Chumps*."

If you omit a full sentence or more from within a quoted passage, add a period before the ellipsis. Use an ellipsis at the end of a quotation only when you omit words at the end of the last quoted sentence. (If words are missing at the beginning of a quotation, no ellipsis is necessary.)

> Jackson goes on to explain that "according to Edward Meyer, vice president and archivist of present-day Ripley Entertainment Inc., . . . the *Believe It or Not* title didn't appear until the following year. . . . within a few years it was a regular daily feature. . . . "

The first ellipsis shows that some words are missing within the sentence. The second ellipsis indicates that a full sentence or more is omitted at that spot. The four dots include the period of the omitted sentence. The last ellipsis shows that *feature* is not the last word of that sentence. The four dots include the period at the end of the sentence.

21f The slash   /

The slash is used to separate. Use a slash as follows:

To separate alternatives. Leave no space before and after the slash.

> I appreciate a newscast now and then without a fire and/or a natural disaster.

Use the slash for this purpose sparingly. *His or her* is generally better, for example, than *his/her*.

To separate two or three lines of poetry. Leave a space on each side of the slash.

> Blake's reverence for nature is evident in such lines as "To see a world in a grain of sand / And a heaven in a wild flower."

22 / Manuscript Format

Before writing out a final copy of a manuscript, check to see if your instructor has provided guidelines. Some instructors, for instance, accept only typed or word-processed papers. The following common guidelines for manuscript format include the Modern Language Association (MLA) recommendations and may be used if your instructor hasn't offered others. Where the American Psychological Association (APA) style instructions differ, they are also included. Note that there are various format styles. The MLA style is widely used in English and humanities papers; the APA style is generally used in psychology and social science papers.

22a Materials and general methods

Word-processed papers. Use 20-pound white paper, 8½ by 11 inches, and dark print. If you use a dot matrix printer, use the highest quality print available, often called near-letter quality. If you use continuous sheets of paper, separate the sheets and remove the perforated edges before handing in your paper. If you have a choice of fonts, select one (such as Times or Courier) that resembles typewriter type.

If using a word processor for an APA-style paper, use a 12-point font.

Typed papers. Use 20-pound white typing paper, 8½ by 11 inches. Do not use onionskin, which makes for difficult reading, or erasable paper, which smudges easily. Use a typewriter ribbon with enough ink to provide dark letters. Keep the typewriter keys clean enough for crisp, clear impressions. Use a pen to write in any marks that are not on your typewriter, such as accent marks.

Handwritten papers. Use white, lined paper, 8½ by 11 inches; do not use paper torn from a spiral notebook. Use black or blue ink, and write letters and punctuation marks as clearly as you can, taking care to distinguish between small and capital letters and to show clearly the placement of punctuation marks.

Binding. Unless asked to do otherwise, simply secure the pages with a paper clip.

22b Text layout

Margins and spacing. In MLA style, leave an inch on all four sides of each page. On word-processed or typed papers, double-space throughout, and print on only one side of the paper. On handwritten papers, write on only one side of the page and on only every other line. Try to avoid dividing words at the end of a line, but if you must divide a word, follow the guidelines in 21a, page 32.

The first line of a paragraph should be indented a half inch (or for typed papers, five spaces) from the left margin.

Quotations of more than four lines of prose or three lines of poetry should be indented one inch (or ten typed spaces) from the left margin. Continue to double-space, both between the preceding text and the quotation and also within the quotation. If you quote all or part of only one paragraph, do not further indent the first line of the quotation. If you quote more than one paragraph, indent the first line of each paragraph another quarter inch (or three typed spaces). However, do not indent the first paragraph if you have omitted its first sentence. (For an example of an indented quotation in the MLA style, see 37a, page 59.)

In the APA style, use margins that are at least an inch, and indent paragraphs five to seven spaces. Do not divide words at the end of a line. Start a quotation of forty words or more on a new line and indent it five to seven spaces from the left margin. Even if the quotation begins at the start of a paragraph, do not indent the first sentence. However, indent the first line of each additional paragraph an additional five to seven spaces. (For an example of an indented quotation in the APA style, see 38a, page 65.)

Heading and title. According to MLA guidelines, there's no need for a title page unless your instructor requests one, in which case, use your instructor's guidelines. Otherwise, beginning at the left margin an inch from the top of the first page, write on separate double-spaced lines the four parts of the heading: your name, the instructor's name, the course name and number, and the date.

Double-space once after the heading, and then center the title of your paper, double-spacing it if it takes more than one line. Do not use quotation marks around the title or put a period after it. Capitalize the first and last words of the title (and any subtitle) and all other words except for articles (*a, an,* and *the*), coordinating conjunctions (*and, but, so, for, yet, or,* and *nor*), prepositions (such as *about, between, in,* and *to*), and the *to* that is part of an infinitive (such as *to work*). Then double-space again, and begin the text of the paper. Also include on that page the page number with your name before it (see "Page numbers" below).

The APA style calls for a title page. If your instructor wants you to use one, he or she may provide you with instructions on what information to include. Otherwise, do the following: Beginning about a third of the way down the page, write on separate double-spaced and centered lines the title of the paper, your name, the instructor's name, the course name and number, and the date. If your title should run to two lines, continue to double-space it. Also include on the title page the page header and number (see "Page numbers" below).

If you are required to write an abstract, write that on page 2. Then begin your text on page 3; center the title on that page as well. Your instructor may ask you to use headings throughout your paper as a way of providing your reader with an overview of the paper's organization.

Page numbers. For a paper in the MLA style, number each page, including the first, with an Arabic number (1, 2, 3, and so on) flush with the right margin about one-half inch below the top edge. Do not use periods, parentheses, or any other symbol with the number. Write your last name just before each page number.

The Top of Page 1 of an MLA Research Paper

Watkins 1

Paul Watkins
Professor Josephs
English 101
12 May 1995
Corporal Punishment: The Unintended Effects
Natalie Owens was watching Oprah Winfrey and preparing dinner while Lucas, age five, and Doug, three, played quietly in the back yard. Suddenly, a blood-curdling scream

If you use the APA style, begin numbering the pages with the title page. Use Arabic numbers, and place each flush with the right margin somewhere between the top of the paper and the first line of text. Write the first two or three words of the title either above the number or five spaces to the left of it.

The Top of the First Page of Text of an APA Research Paper

Corporal Punishment 3

Corporal Punishment: The Unintended Effects
Natalie Owens was watching Oprah Winfrey and preparing dinner while Lucas, age five, and Doug, three, played quietly in the back yard. Suddenly, a blood-curdling

Typing punctuation. Space once after a comma, a semicolon, a colon, any mark of punctuation at the end of a sentence, and between ellipses dots. (Some instructors may prefer you to space twice after a colon or an end mark.) Form a dash by typing two hyphens with no space between them; there should be no space before or after the dash.

List of sources. The style and layout of sources used in your paper are explained in "Documentation" on pages 59–64 (for a paper using the MLA style) or pages 65–68 (for a paper in the APA style).

22c Proofreading and making corrections

Before handing in your paper, proofread it carefully for errors in typing, layout, spelling, punctuation, and grammar. For suggestions on proofreading, see 33b, Step 5, page 54.

You can eliminate all or most of your errors on a self-correcting typewriter or a word processor. Other errors can be eliminated with white correction fluid. Many instructors will allow you to cross out errors, with the correction neatly typed or written above. Draw in a caret (∧) to show where the correction is inserted. Any page with numerous corrections should be retyped.

23 / Capital Letters

Following are guidelines for using capital letters. If after checking these points you are still unsure about whether to capitalize a particular word, a good dictionary may provide the answer.

Capitalize the following:

23a The first word in a sentence or direct quotation

Sentences, including those in direct quotations, begin with capital letters.

The ice cream man said, "Try a frozen banana bar. They're delicious."

"I'm sure they are," the woman replied, "but they're too hard for my dentures."

In the last sentence, the word *but* is not capitalized because it does not start a sentence. It is part of the sentence that begins with the words *I'm sure they are.*

Exception: Do not capitalize the first word of a quoted sentence that is blended into the rest of the sentence: Casey Stengel recalled about Babe Ruth that "he had good stuff, a good fastball, a fine curve—a dipsy-do that made you think a little."

23b The first word of an independent clause that follows a colon

When an independent clause follows a colon, capitalizing the first word after the colon is optional. Capitalize when what follows the colon is a question, a lengthy statement, or a point you wish to emphasize.

There is one thing that all people who accomplish a lot do: They [*or* they] organize their time.

Note: Do not capitalize the first word after a colon unless it begins an independent clause.

When studying class notes, don't forget the last step: testing yourself.

23c The word *I*

Capitalize the word *I* even when it doesn't begin a sentence.

Although I'm fond of Mei Ling, I don't care for her husband.

23d Titles

Capitalize the titles of works, including books, magazines, articles, stories, papers, poems, TV and stage shows, movies, and songs. Articles (*a*, *an*, and *the*), short prepositions (such as *of* and *to*), and coordinating conjunctions (such as *and* and *but*) are not capitalized unless they are the first or last word of the title.

Sitting in the waiting room, the man nervously paged through issues of **Life** and **People** magazines.

Gwen wrote a paper titled "**A V**iew of **A**frican-**A**merican **W**omen," which was based on the book and movie *The Color Purple.*

For information on when to set titles off with quotation marks and when to italicize (or underline) them, see 20b, page 31, and 24a, page 37.

23e Opening and closing of a letter

Capitalize all words in the salutation of a letter.

Dear Ms. Axelrod: **Dear S**ir or **M**adam:

Capitalize only the first word of the closing of a letter.

Sincerely yours,   **Y**ours truly,

23f Abbreviations

Capitalize radio and television station call letters and abbreviations of organizations, government agencies, and companies. Also capitalize certain acronyms (words formed from the initials of a name).

KUOM-FM   KYW-TV   NAACP   NASA   IBM   NATO

23g Proper nouns and adjectives

Capitalize **proper nouns**—the names of specific persons, places, or things. Do not capitalize **common nouns**—all other nouns.

Proper Nouns	Common Nouns
Eve	woman
Thomas Edison	inventor
Canada	country
Philadelphia	city
Olympia College	college
Mars	planet
Titanic	ship

Do not capitalize common nouns even to give them special emphasis or added importance.

Incorrect: The *C*ollege is near the *S*tate *C*apital.
Correct: The *c*ollege is near the *s*tate *c*apital.

Also capitalize all **proper adjectives**, adjectives that are formed from proper nouns.

Canadian provinces   **I**talian cruise ship

Following are types of proper nouns:

People's names and titles used as part of their names

Mayor **A**nderson spoke to **O**fficer **J**enkins after the burglary.
Ethan **B**rown, **J**r., and **P**rofessor **I**rma **S**tone will speak at the student union this evening.

Do not capitalize a title that is not used as part of a person's name.

Irma **S**tone, **p**rofessor of **e**ducation, will retire this year.

However, usage varies for titles of high distinction.

The **P**resident [*or* **p**resident] held a press conference this afternoon.

Family words used as names or as part of names

Go help **G**randfather carry those heavy bags.
Phil is staying at **U**ncle **R**aymond's house for the holidays.

Note: Do not capitalize words such as *grandfather* when they come after possessive words such as *my*, *her*, or *your*:
My **g**randmother lives next door to your **p**arents.

Names for the deity, religions, religious followers, and sacred books

There are various names for **G**od, including the **A**lmighty, **J**ehovah, and **A**llah.
The native religion of Japan is **S**hintoism.
The **K**oran is the sacred text of **I**slam.

Races, nationalities, tribes and languages

The term *Caucasian* was used until recently to refer to a member of a particular racial division.
Karol, who is a **P**olish-**A**merican, can speak **C**hinese and **R**ussian.

Exception: The racial terms *black* and *white* may be capitalized, but often are not.

Specific places (such as countries, cities, bodies of water, streets, buildings, and parks)

Ms. Evans, who is the president of a bank in **B**oston, grew up on a farm near **K**okomo, **I**ndiana.
Neighborhood children pretend that the pond on **F**arwell **A**venue is the **P**acific **O**cean.

Note: Places that are not specifically named should not be capitalized: Ms. Evans, who is president of a bank in a **b**ig **c**ity, grew up on a farm near a **s**mall **c**ity.

Specific organizations (such as government agencies, educational institutions, businesses, political parties, courts, and civic groups)

The **G**overnment **A**ccounting **O**ffice found numerous cases of over-billing the government.
The local president of **M**others **A**gainst **D**runk **D**riving is a part-time real estate agent for **H**ometown **R**ealty.

Days of the week, months, and holidays

At first, **T**hanksgiving was celebrated on the last **T**hursday in **N**ovember, but it was later changed to the fourth **T**hursday of the month.

Note: The names of the seasons (spring, summer, fall, winter) are not capitalized: The children love **f**all and **w**inter because their favorite holidays occur then.

Brand names (but not the kind of product)

Every morning Mario has **M**inute **M**aid orange juice and **S**pecial **K** cereal with milk.

Specific school courses

This semester, Jody is taking **D**ance 101, **G**eneral **P**sychology, and **E**conomics 235.

Note: The names of general subject areas are not capitalized (except for languages): This semester, Jody is taking a **g**ym class, a **p**sychology course, and an **e**conomics class.

Historical periods, well-known events, and documents

During the **M**iddle **A**ges, only the nobility and the clergy could read and write.
The act of protest in which 342 tea chests were thrown into the ocean came to be known as the **B**oston **T**ea **P**arty.
The **M**agna **C**arta, the charter of English liberties, was granted in 1215.

24 / Italics (Underlining)

Italics is a typeface slanted to the right (*like this*) used for certain purposes in printed material. In typewritten or handwritten material, underlining is used instead.

24a Italicize or underline the following:

Titles of separate works

Books. Over 20 million copies have been sold of *Gone with the Wind*.

Magazines. The children's magazine *Cricket* is available at the library.

Newspapers. We buy the *New York Times* on Sundays.

> **Note:** The word *the* is not capitalized or italicized in the title of a newspaper or magazine—even if *the* is part of the title on the publication.

Plays. After almost four hundred years, people are still not tired of *Hamlet*.

Long poems. In *Paradise Lost*, John Milton tries to explain the prevalence of evil.

Comic strips. The characters in *Peanuts* have become part of our culture.

Films. Some movie fans can recite long passages from *Casablanca*.

TV and radio programs. Thirty-nine half-hour episodes were filmed of *The Honeymooners*.

Paintings and sculptures. The portrait titled *Mona Lisa* is of a young woman with a charming smile.

Computer software. People in our office use *WordPerfect*.

Names of specific ships, aircraft, and spacecraft

The *Titanic* sank on its very first voyage.

Foreign words used in English sentences

My French instructor calls me *mademoiselle*.

> **Note:** Many foreign words, such as *burrito* and *karate*, are so widely used and understood that they have become part of the English language and should not be italicized. In general, if a foreign word is listed in an English dictionary, it is considered to have been absorbed into English.

Words, letters, and numbers referred to as such

When *d* and *g* are paired in a word, as in *fudge*, they have the sound of *j*.

Written on the front of the envelope was the number *4*.

24b Italicize for emphasis.

Use italics for this purpose rarely. It is generally better to find words that, through their meaning and order, provide the emphasis you seek.

Marie replied, "I don't believe *you*."

24c Do not italicize (or put quotation marks around) the following:

The title of a paper (except for words that would otherwise be italicized, such as the words in a title of a novel)

Characterization in *The Scarlet Letter*

Titles of major sacred works, such as the Bible and books in it

Genesis is the first book of the **Old Testament**.

Names of legal documents

The first ten amendments to the **U.S. Constitution** are called the **Bill of Rights**.

25 / Numbers

In formal writing for the general reader, follow the guidelines below.

25a Spell out any number that can be written in one or two words; otherwise, use numerals.

When written out, numbers twenty-one through ninety-nine are hyphenated.

> When my grandmother turned **sixty-nine**, she went on a **fifteen**-day trip across nine states.
>
> The mail carrier delivered **512** pieces of mail today.

> **Exception:** When one or more numbers in a series need to be written as numerals, use numerals for the entire series: The movie theater sold **137** tickets to a horror movie, **64** to a comedy, and **17** to a romance.

25b Spell out any number that begins a sentence.

Eight hundred and seventy-one dollars was found in the briefcase.

> **Note:** To avoid writing out a long number, you can rewrite the sentence: The briefcase contained **$871**.

25c Use numerals for the following:

Dates

My grandfather was born on July **4**, **1909**.

> **Note:** Do not use such forms as *1st*, *2nd*, *3rd*, and *4th* in dates unless the year is not given: The deadline is November **10th**.

Times of the day

The last guest left at **1:45** a.m.

> **Exception:** When the word *o'clock* is used, the time is spelled out: I got home at **six o'clock**.

> **Note:** Spell out the numbers when describing amounts of time: I worked **fifty** hours last week.

Addresses

The bookstore is located at **1216** North **48th** Street.

Identification numbers (TV channel numbers, radio dial numbers, room numbers, serial numbers, road numbers, and so on)

For highway information, turn to **102.3** on your radio dial.

Fractions and decimals

The answers are **33⅓** and **4.555**.

Note: Fractions less than one are often written in words: **one-half, a third**.

Percentages

Nearly **70** percent of the class donated blood.

Pages and divisions of books and plays

Please read act **1**, scene **3** of the play, on pages **10–15**.

Exact amounts of money

The restaurant bill came to **$8.49**.

The parking ticket cost **$50**.

Scores and statistics

The New York Knicks beat the Indiana Pacers **94–90**.

People with an IQ between **20** and **35** are considered severely retarded.

According to one survey, **6** out of **10** residents in town are against building the mall.

Exact measurements

The kitchen table is a square—**4** feet by **4** feet.

In very large round numbers

Earth is **93** million miles from the sun.

25d When writing numerals, use commas to indicate thousands.

Angie has **1,243** pennies in a jar.

The number that comes after **999,999** is **1,000,000**.

Exceptions: Do not use commas in telephone numbers (**555-1234**), street numbers (**3244** Oak Street), zip codes (**08043**), Social Security numbers (**372-45-0985**), or years (**1996**).

26 / Abbreviations

26a Abbreviations for the following are appropriate in formal writing:

Titles that are used before and after people's names

Ms. Glenda Oaks   Keith Rodham, **Sr.**
Dr. Jim Huang   Marcia Jamison, **LL.D.**
Rev. Thomas Ball   Samuel Farmer, **M.D.**

Note 1: Do not use two titles at one time that mean the same thing.

Incorrect: *Dr.* Ellen Steinman, *M.D.*
Correct: **Dr.** Ellen Steinman *or* Ellen Steinman, **M.D.**

Note 2: Spell out titles that are not used with a person's name.

Incorrect: The *prof.* is out of town this week.
Correct: The **professor** is out of town this week.

Initials in a person's name

Daphne **A.** Miller   **T.** Martin Sawyer

Specific time and date references

The exam ended at 4:45 **p.m.**

Cleopatra lived from about 69 to 30 **B.C.** (*or* 69 to 30 **B.C.E.**—"Before the Common Era")

Muslims calculate their calendar from Friday, July 16, **A.D.** 622 (*or* 622 **C.E.**—"the Common Era")

Note: Do not use time and date abbreviations without a number:

Incorrect: The airplane should land in the *a.m.*
Correct: The airplane should land in the **morning**.

Organizations, agencies, countries, and corporations known by their initials, and acronyms (words formed from the initials of a name). These are usually written in all capital letters and without periods.

YMCA   FBI   USA   NBC   AIDS

A long name that is used often in a paper may be abbreviated as follows: When using the name the first time, use the full name followed by the abbreviation in parentheses. From that point on, you may use only the abbreviation.

The Irish Republican Army (**IRA**) declared war against British rule in 1969.

Latin words. Abbreviations of Latin words (such as those below) are often considered appropriate only in scholarly, technical, and formal writing. In informal writing, use Latin abbreviations parenthetically and sparingly.

Some flowers that do well in shade (**e.g.**, impatiens) provide color all summer.

In formal writing, limit your use of such abbreviations to footnotes and bibliographies.

Latin abbreviation	*English meaning*
e.g. (for *exempli gratia*)	for example
et al. (for *et alii*)	and others
etc. (for *et cetera*)	and so forth
i.e. (for *id est*)	that is
N.B. (for *nota bene*)	note well

26b In formal writing, do not abbreviate the following:

Personal names

Incorrect: *Geo.* Washington's first inauguration was in 1789.
Correct: **George** Washington's first inauguration was in 1789.

States and countries

Incorrect: The company's headquarters are in *Mpls., Minn.*
Correct: The company's headquarters are in **Minneapolis, Minnesota**.

Days of the week and months

Incorrect: We're moving on the first *Mon.* in *Dec.*
Correct: We're moving on the first **Monday** in **December**.

Holidays

Incorrect: The Whitman brothers are going home for *Xmas.*
Correct: The Whitman brothers are going home for **Christmas.**

School courses

Incorrect: The professor is teaching a class in *ab. psych.* this semester.
Correct: The professor is teaching a class in **abnormal psychology** this semester.

Parts of written works

Incorrect: Turn to the first *p.* of the first *chpt.*
Correct: Turn to the first **page** of the first **chapter**.

Units of measurement

Incorrect: One *lb.* equals sixteen *ozs.*
Correct: One **pound** equals sixteen **ounces**.

27 / Spelling Improvement

When you are developing the content of a paper, it may be difficult to pay attention to spelling. For that reason, it is important to spend a few minutes proofreading your final drafts for spelling errors. Pay attention to every word, not just the ones that are difficult to spell. Assuming that "easy" words are spelled correctly often leads to such errors as *to* for *too* or *beleive* for *believe*.

In addition, you can improve your spelling by using the hints and rules that follow.

27a Use the dictionary.

The single most important way to improve your spelling is to get into the habit of checking words in a dictionary. You may ask, "If I can't spell a word, how can I find it in the dictionary?" The answer is that you have to guess what the letters might be. Here are some hints to help you make informed guesses.

Hint 1. If you're not sure about the vowels in a word, you will have to experiment. Vowels often sound the same, so try an *i* in place of an *a*, an *e* in place of an *i*, and so on.

Hint 2. Consonants are sometimes doubled in a word. If you can't find your word with single consonants, try doubling them.

Hint 3. Following are groups of letters or letter combinations that often sound alike. If your word isn't spelled with one of the letters in a pair or group shown below, it might be spelled with another in the same pair or group. For example, if it isn't spelled with a *k*, it may be spelled with a *c*, *ch*, or *ck*.

Vowels				
ai / ay	**au / aw**	**ee / ea**	**ou / ow**	**oo / u**
Consonants				
c / k / ch / ck	**c / s**	**f / ph**	**g / j**	**sch / sc / sk** **s / z**
Combinations				
re / ri	**able / ible**	**ent / ant**	**er / or**	**tion / sion**

27b Use an electronic spelling checker.

Take advantage of electronic spelling tools. If you work on a computer or electronic typewriter that has a spelling checker, use it before finalizing your papers. Pocket-sized electronic spelling checkers are also widely available.

However, even if you have an electronic spelling-check program, you will still need to proofread your papers for spelling errors. Spelling programs cannot correct words that are not in their word list. Also, they cannot differentiate between commonly confused words, such as *affect* and *effect* or *their* and *there*.

27c Keep a personal spelling list.

In a special place, write down every word you misspell. Include its correct spelling, underline the difficult part of the word, and add any hints you can use to remember how to spell it. If spelling is a particular problem for you, you might even want to start a spelling notebook that has a separate page for each letter of the alphabet. Here's one format you might use:

How I spelled it	*Correct spelling*	*Hints*
recieve	rec<u>ei</u>ve	I before E except after C
seperate	sep<u>a</u>rate	There's A RAT in sep**ARAT**e
alot	<u>a</u> lot	Two words (like "a little")
alright	<u>all</u> right	Two words (like "all wrong")

Study your list regularly, and refer to it whenever you write and proofread a paper.

27d Learn commonly confused words.

Many spelling errors result from words that sound alike or almost alike but that are spelled differently, such as *brake* and *break*, *wear* and *where*, or *right* and *write*. To avoid such errors, study carefully the commonly confused words in the "Glossary of Usage" on pages 41–47.

27e Learn some helpful spelling rules.

Even poor spellers can improve by following a few spelling rules. On the next page are rules that apply to many words.

I before E rule. Put *i* before *e* except after *c* or when sounded like *a*, as in *neighbor* and *weigh*.

I *before* e	*Except after* c	*Or when sounded like* a
belief, chief, field	receive, ceiling	vein, eight

Exceptions to the above rule include: either, leisure, foreign, science, society

Silent E rule. If a word ends in a silent (unpronounced) *e*, drop the *e* before adding an ending that starts with a vowel. Keep the *e* when adding an ending that begins with a consonant.

Drop the e *with endings that start with a vowel*	*Keep the* e *with endings that start with a consonant*
like + ed = liked	love + ly = lovely
confuse + ing = confusing	shame + ful = shameful
fame + ous = famous	hope + less = hopeless
guide + ance = guidance	base + ment = basement

Exceptions include: noticeable, argument, judgment, truly

Y rule. Change the final *y* of a word to *i* before adding an ending when

a the last two letters of the word are a consonant plus *y*,

b and the ending being added begins with a vowel or is *-ful, -ly,* or *-ness.*

Exception: Keep the *y* if the ending being added is *-ing.*

Change the y *to* i	*Keep the* y
try + ed = tried	try + ing = trying
carry + er = carrier	carry + ing = carrying
beauty + ful = beautiful	gray + ed = grayed
lucky + ly = luckily	display + ed = displayed
happy + ness = happiness	destroy + s = destroys

Doubling rule. Double the final consonant of a word before adding an ending when

a the last three letters of the word are a consonant, a vowel, and a consonant (CVC),

b the word is only one syllable (for example, *stop*) or is accented on the last syllable (for example, *begin*),

c and the ending being added begins with a vowel.

One-syllable words that end in CVC	*Words accented on the last syllable that end in CVC*
stop + ed = stopped	begin + ing = beginning
flat + er = flatter	control + er = controller
red + est = reddest	occur + ence = occurrence

Rules for adding *-es* to nouns and verbs that end in *s, sh, ch,* or *x*. Most plurals are formed by adding *-s* to the singular noun (*roses, skates, hurricanes*). However, for nouns that end in *s, sh, ch,* or *x,* form the plural by adding *-es.*

kiss + es = kisses	coach + es = coaches
wish + es = wishes	tax + es = taxes

Most third-person singular verbs end in *-s* (*he runs, she sings, it grows*). However, for verbs that end in *s, sh, ch,* or *x,* form the third-person singular with *-es.*

miss + es = misses	catch + es = catches
wash + es = washes	mix + es = mixes

Rules for adding *-es* to nouns and verbs that end in a consonant plus y. For nouns that end in a consonant plus *y,* form the plural by changing the *y* to *i* and adding *-es.*

fly + es = flies	lady + es = ladies
canary + es = canaries	

For verbs that end in a consonant plus *y,* form the third-person singular by changing the *y* to *i* and adding *-es.*

pity + es = pities	marry + es = marries
bully + es = bullies	

27f Learn commonly misspelled words.

Following are one hundred common words that are frequently misspelled. To master them, have someone drill you on them, and then practice the words that you misspelled.

	absence		embarrassment		permanent
	accommodate		emphasize	70	perseverance
	acknowledge		enthusiasm		persistent
	acquaintance		environment		persuade
	acquire		exaggerate		physically
	across	40	exercise		preference
	amateur		existence		prejudice
	analyze		fascinate		prevalent
	apparently		guarantee		privilege
10	appropriate		guidance		procedure
	argument		height		procedure
	association		hypocrisy	80	pronunciation
	beginning		imaginary		psychology
	beneficial		independent		recommend
	business		indispensable		reference
	calendar	50	inevitable		repetition
	characteristic		irrelevant		restaurant
	committee		irresistible		rhythm
	competitive		legitimate		ridiculous
20	condemn		maintenance		schedule
	conscience		maneuver		secretary
	continuous		mathematics	90	separate
	convenient		mischievous		similar
	courteous		necessary		sophomore
	criticism		noticeable		succeed
	curiosity	60	obstacle		summary
	definitely		occasionally		surprise
	description		occurred		tendency
	desperate		omission		thorough
30	disastrous		opportunity		tragedy
	discipline		optimistic		unnecessary
	efficient		original	100	usually
	eighth		parallel		
	eligible		particularly		

28 / Glossary of Usage

This glossary can help you choose the correct word (or spelling) as you write. The frequently misused or confused words listed here fall into several categories. Some are pairs of words that are similar in pronunciation but different in meaning and spelling. Others have meanings or uses that are widely misunderstood. Still others are considered **colloquial** (acceptable for informal use only) or **nonstandard** (not acceptable in most writing and speech, both formal and informal).

a, an. Use *a* before a word that begins with a consonant sound: **a h**arp, **a p**hotograph, **a u**niform (the *u* is pronounced as though it were preceded by *y*). Use *an* before a word beginning with a vowel sound: **an e**lephant, **an h**onor (the *h* is silent), **an u**ncle.

accept, except. *Accept* is a verb that means "to receive (something that's offered)." *Except* is usually a preposition that means "excluding."

> Did he **accept** the apology?
> All the furniture was sold **except** the rocking chair.

adapt, adopt. *Adapt* means "to adjust (to new conditions)." *Adopt* means "to take as one's own."

> The lion cub that was raised by humans could not **adapt** to life in the wild.
> The Vietnamese family soon **adopted** many American customs.

advice, advise. *Advice* is a noun that means "guidance" or "counsel." *Advise* is a verb that means "to give advice."

> The first-year student sought a senior's **advice** on course selection.
> The senior **advised** her to sample courses from several areas of interest.

affect, effect. *Affect* is usually used as a verb that means "to influence." *Effect* is usually a noun meaning "a result."

> The crash of the stock market **affected** the entire country.
> The **effects** of the stock market crash included mass unemployment and hunger.

all ready, already. *All ready* means "completely prepared." *Already* means "previously."

> Dinner was **all ready**.
> I had eaten **already**.

allusion, illusion. *Allusion* means "indirect reference." *Illusion* means "erroneous belief" or "false impression."

> The former enemies made no reference, not even an **allusion**, to their previous disagreement.
> The **illusion** that Mr. Casey cared about me has been shattered.
> Cathedral windows gave the room the **illusion** of great height.

almost, most. See *most*.

a lot, alot. *A lot* is colloquial when used to mean "many" or "much" and should be avoided in formal writing. *Alot* is a misspelling of *a lot*.

alright. Nonstandard spelling of *all right*.

altogether, all together. *Altogether* means "entirely." *All together* means "in a group."

> The movie is **altogether** too violent for children.
> The wedding gifts were **all together** in the dining room.

among, between. See *between, among*.

amoral, immoral. *Amoral* means "not concerned with moral judgments." *Immoral* means "morally wrong."

> The tiger feels no hatred for the animals it kills; its actions are entirely **amoral**.
> Murder, rape, and robbery are all **immoral** acts.

amount, number. Use *amount* when referring to things in bulk or mass that cannot be counted. Use *number* when referring to countable things.

> Only a small **amount** of oatmeal is left.
> There are a **number** of scratches on the table.

and/or. Use only when you mean to indicate three options—the first alternative mentioned, the second alternative mentioned, or both.

> The fault lies with the surgeon **and/or** the hospital staff.

If you mean either one alternative or the other, use *or*. If you mean both, use *and*.

> The fault lies with either the surgeon **or** the hospital staff.
> The fault lies with the surgeon **and** the hospital staff.

A common conservative view of *and/or* is that it should be used only in legal, technical, and business writing.

anxious, eager. *Anxious* means "worried." *Eager* means "impatiently desirous."

> The patient's family was **anxious** about the results of the brain scan.
> Band members were **eager** to see their new uniforms.

anymore, any more. *Anymore* means "any longer" or "at present." *Any more* means "additional."

> Alice doesn't live here **anymore**.
> Is there **any more** coffee?

anyone, any one. *Anyone* means "any person." *Any one* refers to a single one of a number of people or items.

> I don't know **anyone** from Arkansas.
> **Any one** of the guests could have murdered Colonel Mustard.

anyplace. Colloquial. In formal writing, use *anywhere*.

> Many people don't go **anywhere** [not *anyplace*] without their credit cards.

anyways, anywheres. Nonstandard for *anyway* and *anywhere*.

as. Do not use *as* to mean "because" if there is any chance of ambiguity about whether it shows cause and effect or time.

> I stepped out of the shower **because** [not *as*, which in this case could also mean *when*] the phone rang.

as, like. In formal writing, use only *as* or *as if* [not *like*] to introduce a dependent clause. *Like* is a preposition and in formal usage should be followed only by a noun or noun phrase.

> No worker is as dedicated **as** [not *like*] Mac is.
>
> The wrestler looks **as if** [not *like*] he could tear his opponent limb from limb.
>
> The bush looks **like** a tree.

assure, ensure, insure. *Assure* means "to convince or promise." *Ensure* and *insure* mean "to make sure or safe" and are generally interchangeable. However, only *insure* is used for references to insurance policies.

> They **assured** us that they would meet us at the airport.
>
> We left early to **ensure** [or **insure**] that we would get to the airport on time.
>
> Fred Astaire's legs were **insured** by Lloyd's of London.

awful, awfully. *Awful* is an adjective that means "awe-inspiring." The use of *awful* to mean "terrible" is colloquial and therefore inappropriate in formal writing. The use of the adverb *awfully* as an intensifier (*awfully good*, *awfully late*) is also colloquial.

> The early settlers were amazed by the **awful** peaks of the Rocky Mountains.
>
> The guest of honor had a **terrible** [not an *awful*] headache.
>
> The river was **very** [not *awfully*] polluted.

a while, awhile. *A while* is an article and a noun; in that form, *while* can function as a subject or object. *Awhile*, an adverb, can modify verbs.

> **A while** passed before the rain stopped.
>
> He waited for **a while**.
>
> We chatted **awhile**.

bad, badly. *Bad* is an adjective and can follow a linking verb. *Badly* is an adverb and modifies an action verb.

> The weather is **bad**.
>
> The guitarist played **badly**.
>
> (See also "Adjectives and Adverbs," pages 16–17.)

being as, being that. Considered colloquial or nonstandard. Use *because* or *since*.

> **Since** [not *being as* or *being that*] our guest used a wheelchair, we arranged to have a ramp at the front door.

beside, besides. *Beside* means "at the side of." *Besides* means "in addition to." *Besides* can also mean "except."

> The table **beside** the bed is very old.
>
> **Besides** being unkind, your statement is untrue.
>
> Few people **besides** his wife know Mr. Morris well.

between, among. Use *between* for two people or things. Use *between* for three or more when they are considered as distinct individuals or items. Use *among* for three or more people or things when they are considered collectively or as a mass.

> The wedding guests could choose **between** a chicken and a salmon entree.
>
> The executive's job keeps him traveling **between** New York, Chicago, and Los Angeles.
>
> There is a feeling **among** the workers that the company does not have their welfare at heart.
>
> Wild green onions are growing **among** the marigolds.

brake, break. *Brake* means "to slow or to stop" or "the part of a vehicle used to slow or stop it"; *break* means "to cause to come apart" or "a temporary stop or rest."

> If you get a **break** from your work, could you check the **brake** on my bike?

bring, take. Use *bring* for something being moved toward the speaker. Use *take* for something being moved away from the speaker.

> When you come over, please **bring** your class notes.
>
> **Take** the garbage out after supper.

bursted, bust, busted. *Bursted* is a nonstandard form of the irregular verb *burst*, and *bust* and *busted* are slang forms of the verb. The principal parts of *burst* are *burst*, *burst*, and *burst*.

> These balloons **burst** easily. Yesterday, the balloon **burst** suddenly. Most of the balloons had already **burst**.

can, may. In formal usage, *can* means "to be able" and *may* means "to have permission."

> **Can** you drive a car?
>
> **May** I borrow your car?

capital, capitol. As a noun, *capital* means "the city or town that is the seat of government in a state or country" or "wealth used or gained in business." *Capitol* is the building in which a legislature meets.

> The **capital** of Minnesota is St. Paul.
>
> One needs substantial **capital** to finance a fast-food restaurant.
>
> The dome of the **capitol** can be seen for miles.

cite, site. *Cite* is a verb that means "to quote as an authority or an example" or "to mention as an example or proof." *Site* means "the place where something is or was located."

> In his paper on mental illness, the student **cited** his father, a psychiatrist.
>
> To support her point, the lawyer **cited** a previous case.
>
> The tour guide said this was the **site** of a Civil War battle.

classic, classical. *Classic* means "of the highest class" or "serving as a model or standard." *Classical* means "relating to the art and culture of ancient Greece and Rome." *Classical music* refers to music in the European tradition, such as symphonies and operas.

> *Death of a Salesman* is a **classic** example of American drama.
>
> The **classical** dimensions of the Parthenon in Athens are still admired by architects today.

coarse, course. *Coarse* refers to a roughness of texture or conduct. *Course* refers to a path or a unit of studies.

> The fabric was a **coarse** wool.
>
> The cowboy's manners were **coarse**.
>
> The river's **course** was snakelike.
>
> I'm taking a math **course**.

compare to, compare with. Use *compare to* when you are pointing out similarities between two people or things. Use *compare with* when you are pointing out similarities and differences between two people or things.

The young playwright is being **compared to** Neil Simon.

The assignment is to **compare** *Romeo and Juliet* **with** *West Side Story*.

complement, compliment. *Complement* means "to complete or make perfect." *Compliment* means "to praise or flatter."

The red scarf **complements** your outfit.

The instructor **complimented** Stan on his essay.

conscience, conscious. *Conscience* means "the sense of right and wrong." *Conscious* means "aware."

The lie he had told bothered the boy's **conscience**.

The server was **conscious** of the diners' impatience.

continual, continuous. *Continual* implies regular or frequent repetition. *Continuous* implies a continuing without interruption.

That dog's **continual** barking has annoyed the neighbors for weeks.

Luckily, the force of gravity is **continuous**.

could care less. Nonstandard for *couldn't care less*.

could of. Nonstandard for *could have*.

council, counsel, consul. A *council* is a group of people assembled to consider and make decisions on issues. *Counsel* means "advice" or "attorney." A *consul* is a government official who is stationed in a foreign country.

The city **council** will decide whether parking meters will be installed on Main Street.

Ryan's children often turn to him for **counsel**.

The defense **counsel** objected to five questions in a row.

The President is having dinner with the Italian **consul**.

course, coarse. See *coarse, course*.

criteria, criterion. *Criteria* is the plural of *criterion*, which means "a standard on which a judgment or decision can be based."

There is only one **criterion** for membership in that club, money.

Companies are not allowed to use age and race as **criteria** for hiring or firing people.

data. *Data* means "factual information." Since it is the plural of *datum*, some experts feel that *data* must always take a plural verb.

The data **lead** [not *leads*] us to conclude that inflation is on the rise.

However, many experts and writers feel that *data* should be treated as a singular noun when it refers to a single collection of information:

The little data we have **is** [not *are*] not sufficient to come to a conclusion.

device, devise. *Device* is a noun that means "a mechanical invention." *Devise* is a verb that means "to plan or invent."

This **device** allows deaf people to communicate over the telephone.

The jewel thief **devised** a way to enter the museum without tripping the alarm.

different from, different than. Generally, use *different from*. However, if the object of comparison is stated in a clause, use *than*.

Happiness is **different from** joy.

Our weekends are different **than** they used to be.

disinterested, uninterested. *Disinterested* means "impartial." *Uninterested* means "not interested."

A judge must be **disinterested**.

The class is dull because the instructor is so **uninterested** in her subject.

each and every. Redundant; use either *each* or *every*.

eager, anxious. See *anxious, eager*.

effect, affect. See *affect, effect*.

e.g. Latin abbreviation of words meaning "for example" or "for instance." In formal writing, use the English equivalents except in footnotes.

elicit, illicit. *Elicit* is a verb that means "to draw forth." *Illicit* is an adjective that means "unlawful."

Fireworks always **elicit** admiring gasps from the crowd.

The gangster made his living from prostitution, drugs, and other **illicit** activities.

emigrate, immigrate. *Emigrate* means "to leave a country." *Immigrate* means "to enter a new country."

The Jaffes recently **emigrated** from Russia.

The Jaffes **immigrated** to Israel to join relatives there.

eminent, imminent. *Eminent* means "distinguished in reputation." *Imminent* means "about to happen."

It's an honor to meet such an **eminent** member of Congress.

A fist fight between the two angry boys seemed **imminent**.

ensure, assure, insure. See *assure, ensure, insure*.

enthused. Colloquial. In formal writing, use *enthusiastic*.

He was **enthusiastic** [not *enthused*] about his new job.

etc. Latin abbreviation for a word meaning "and other things." Use *and so forth* or *and others* in formal writing.

everyday, every day. *Everyday* is an adjective meaning "commonplace" or "ordinary." The phrase *every day* functions as either a noun or an adverb meaning "each day."

During exam week, cramming is an **everyday** activity for many students.

Every day is a challenge.

Janet reviews her biology notes **every day**.

everyone, every one. *Everyone* means "every person." *Every one* means "each person or thing of a group."

Everyone wants to be liked.

Every one of the Andersons has the flu.

except, accept. See *accept, except*.

explicit, implicit. *Explicit* means "precisely expressed" or "specific." *Implicit* means "implied, suggested."

> The children were given an **explicit** warning to stay away from the quarry.
>
> Despite the man's friendly words, there was a threat **implicit** in his grim expression.

famous, infamous. *Famous* means "widely known," usually in a favorable sense. *Infamous* means "having a very bad reputation."

> A generation after her death, Marilyn Monroe is still a **famous** movie star.
>
> Bedlam was an **infamous** asylum where the mentally ill were treated like beasts.

farther, further. Use *farther* to refer to distance. Use *further* to mean "more" or "to a greater extent."

> Which is **farther** from here, Montgomery Mall or Woodbury Mall?
>
> The killing of black protesters led to **further** racial tensions in South Africa.

fewer, less. Use *fewer* with items that can be counted (plural nouns). Use *less* with general amounts that are uncountable (singular nouns).

> The hen laid **fewer** eggs today than yesterday.
>
> Many people are eating **less** fat these days.

former, latter. *Former* refers to the first of two items, and *latter* refers to the second of two items. For three or more items, use *first* and *last*.

> Between being too busy or bored, I'll always choose the **former** because I hate the **latter**.

further, farther. See *farther, further*.

good, well. *Good* is an adjective that can follow a linking verb. *Well* is usually an adverb.

> That idea is **good**. This sausage tastes **good**.
>
> The team performed **well** today.
>
> (See also 8b, page 17.)

hanged, hung. Use *hanged* for executions. Use *hung* for all other contexts.

> Most of the famous Western outlaws were finally shot or **hanged**.
>
> Mistletoe was **hung** over the door.

have got. Colloquial. In formal writing, use only *have*.

> We **have** [not *have got*] several volunteers to drive people to the polls.

hisself. Nonstandard for *himself*.

historic, historical. *Historic* is usually used to refer to what is important in history. *Historical* is usually used to refer to anything concerned with history or its study.

> Paul Revere is a **historic** figure in the story of the American Revolution.
>
> *Gone with the Wind* is a **historical** novel set against the background of the Civil War.

hopefully. In its most strict use, *hopefully* means "full of hope."

> The child stared **hopefully** at the chimney, waiting for Santa Claus to appear.

In academic writing, *hopefully* should not be used without telling who is doing the hoping.

> **Environmentalists hope** [not *Hopefully,*] the spotted owl will not have the same fate as the passenger pigeon.

i.e. Latin abbreviation of words meaning *that is*. In formal writing, use *that is*.

illicit, elicit. See *elicit, illicit*.

illusion, allusion. See *allusion, illusion*.

immigrate, emigrate. See *emigrate, immigrate*.

imminent, eminent. See *eminent, imminent*.

immoral, amoral. See *amoral, immoral*.

implicit, explicit. See *explicit, implicit*.

infamous, famous. See *famous, infamous*.

ingenious, ingenuous. *Ingenious* means "clever." *Ingenuous* means "unsophisticated" or "frank."

> One scientist has discovered an **ingenious** way to use water as the main fuel for a car engine.
>
> Having never left home before, Felix was an **ingenuous** traveler.
>
> The student was **ingenuous** enough to admit she didn't like much modern art.

in regards to. Nonstandard for *in regard to* or *as regards* (both of which mean "with reference to").

incredible, incredulous. *Incredible* means "unbelievable" or "hard to believe." *Incredulous* means "unbelieving."

> Their story of surviving a grizzly bear attack is **incredible** but true.
>
> "I accidentally entered the wrong house," the burglar told an **incredulous** police officer.

instance, instant. *Instance* means "an example." As a noun, *instant* means "a brief time." As an adjective, *instant* means "immediate."

> Here's an **instance** of a person going out of his way to help a stranger.
>
> The genie appeared in an **instant**.
>
> This is a crisis demanding **instant** attention.

insure, assure, ensure. See *assure, ensure, insure*.

into, in to. *Into* is a preposition; *in to* is a preposition *(in)* and the first word of an infinitive *(to)*.

> I pulled my car **into** the diner's parking lot and then went **in to** have lunch.

irregardless. Nonstandard version of *regardless*.

is when, is where. Do not use these phrases in definitions.

> A scavenger hunt **is a game in which** [*not* A scavenger hunt *is when* or *is where*] players try to collect unusual items on a list from people in the neighborhood.

its, it's. *Its* is the possessive of the pronoun *it*. *It's* is a contraction of *it is* or *it has*.

> The city of Baltimore lost **its** professional football team when the team moved to Indianapolis.

It's time for a change.

It's been a long time since I've seen you.

kind of, sort of. Colloquial when used to mean *somewhat* or *rather*. Avoid that use in formal writing.

The film's plot is **somewhat** [not **kind of** or **sort of**] confusing.

later, latter. *Later* means "more late." *Latter* means "the second of two persons or things mentioned."

The lazy employee seemed to come in **later** every day.

Given a choice between chocolate and vanilla ice cream, most people prefer the **latter**.

latter, former. See *former, latter*.

lay, lie. *Lay* means "to put" or "to place." It is a transitive verb and therefore always requires an object. Its principal parts are *lay, laid, laid*. *Lie* means "to rest." It is an intransitive verb and therefore never takes an object. Its principal parts are *lie, lay, lain*.

Please **lay** the gun down. She **laid** the gun down. After she had **laid** the gun down, she was arrested.

The dogs **lie** on the couch. The dogs **lay** on the couch all morning. The dogs have never **lain** on the couch before.

lead, led. The verb *lead* (pronounced LEED) means "to guide, conduct, escort, or direct." The verb *led* is the past tense and past participle of the verb *lead*. The noun *lead* (pronounced LED) is a metal.

You can **lead** a horse to water.

Once you have **led** a horse to water, you can't make it drink.

The dental patient wore a **lead** apron to shield against X-rays.

learn, teach. *Learn* means "to gain knowledge of"; *teach* means "to provide knowledge of."

I can **teach** [not *learn*] you some Yiddish if you'd like to **learn** some.

leave, let. *Leave* means "to go away." *Let* means "to allow."

I'm **leaving** on time.

Let the children play until dinnertime.

less, fewer. See *fewer, less*.

liable, likely. *Liable* is generally used to indicate undesirable consequences. *Likely* is used for results that are probable, whether they are desirable or undesirable.

When speaking in public, I am **liable** to shake and stutter.

Since I have studied all semester, I am **likely** to do well on the final.

lie, lay. See *lay, lie*.

like, as. See *as, like*.

loose, lose. *Loose* means "not tight"; *lose* means "to misplace" or "to be deprived of something one has had."

If you don't fix that **loose** steering wheel, you could **lose** control of your car.

lots, lots of. Colloquial when used to mean *many* or *much*. Avoid that use in formal writing.

Many [not *lots* or *lots of*] countries have agreed that Antarctica should remain free from mining until the year 2041.

may, can. See *can, may*.

maybe, may be. *Maybe* is an adverb that means "perhaps." *May be* is a verb phrase.

Maybe you are right. The game **may be** postponed.

may of, might of. Nonstandard for *may have* and *might have*.

media, medium. *Media* is the plural of *medium*, which is used to refer to a means of communication.

No **medium** records history as it happens better than television.

Most **media** depend on advertising for profits.

moral, morale. The adjective *moral* means "ethical." The noun *moral* means "the principle taught by a story," or "standard of behavior." *Morale* is a noun that means "state of mind with respect to confidence and cheerfulness."

Returning the money was the **moral** thing to do.

The **moral** of the story is that you can't please everyone.

He has all the **morals** of a stray tomcat.

The runner's **morale** rose each time she passed a competitor.

most. Colloquial when used to mean *almost*. Avoid that use in formal writing.

Almost [not *Most*] everyone in class passed the course.

nowheres. Nonstandard for *nowhere*.

number, amount. See *amount, number*.

off of. Wordy. Use *off*.

Please get **off** [not *off of*] my bike.

O.K., OK, okay. Colloquial. Use words such as *all right, correct*, or *approve* in formal writing.

The instructor **approved** [not *okayed*] my paper topic.

ought to of. Nonstandard for *ought to have*.

passed, past. *Passed* is a verb that means "went by" or "completed successfully"; *past* is a noun that means "the time before the present."

In the **past**, I **passed** all my courses.

percent, percentage. Use *percent* with a specific number. Otherwise, use *percentage*.

Only 7 **percent** of the people surveyed returned their questionnaires.

What **percentage** of the people returned the questionnaires?

personal, personnel. *Personal* is an adjective that means "private." *Personnel* is a noun that means "employees."

Best friends know each other's most **personal** secrets.

All **personnel** must follow a company dress code.

phenomena, phenomenon. *Phenomena* is the plural of *phenomenon*, which means "an observable fact," "a fact that is unusual or significant," or "a remarkable person."

The rainbow is a delightful **phenomenon** of nature.

There are rumors of strange **phenomena** at a house that is said to be haunted.

Isaac Stern was a musical **phenomenon**.

plenty. Colloquial when used to mean *very* or *quite*. Avoid that use in formal writing.

The instructor was **very** [not *plenty*] interesting.

plus. Do not use *plus* to join independent clauses.

His clothes were dirty, **and** [not *plus*] they were torn.

precede, proceed. *Precede* means "to come before." *Proceed* means "to go forward."

Courtship usually **precedes** marriage.

The train **proceeded** to its destination.

pretty. Colloquial when used to mean *rather* or *quite*. Avoid that use in formal writing.

The patient was feeling **rather** [not *pretty*] strong.

principal, principle. As an adjective, *principal* means "main." As a noun, *principal* means "the person in charge of a school" or "an amount of money borrowed." *Principle* means "a basic truth or guideline."

Her **principal** job is teaching, but she also tutors.

The **principal** of our school once taught English.

A mortgage payment consists of **principal** plus interest.

Our company is based on the **principle** that success results from the customer's satisfaction.

quotation, quote. *Quotation* is a noun. *Quote* is a verb. In formal writing, do not use *quote* as a shortened form of *quotation*.

The film critic's lecture was filled with **quotations** from his favorite movies.

The critic often **quotes** from his favorite movies.

raise, rise. *Raise* means "to lift." It is a transitive verb and therefore requires an object. Its principal parts are *raise, raised, raised*. *Rise* means "to go up." It is an intransitive verb and does not take an object. Its principal parts are *rise, rose, risen*.

Please **raise** the shades. He **raised** his hand in class. We have **raised** the reading level of our school district this year.

Sunflowers **rise** high above the other plants in the garden. The sun **rose** before I woke up. The curtain had already **risen** when we arrived at the theater.

real, really. *Real* is an adjective; *really* is an adverb. The use of *real* to mean *really* (*very, extremely*) is colloquial and should not be used in formal writing.

The firefighter who saved the child was **really** [not *real*] brave.

reason is because. Redundant. Use *that* instead of *because*.

The reason she is late is **that** [not *because*] she had a flat tire.

reason why. Redundant. Use either *reason* or *why*.

I want to know **the reason** [or **why**, but not *the reason why*] you are so late.

respectfully, respectively. *Respectfully* means "in a manner showing respect." *Respectively* means "each in the order mentioned."

A few men **respectfully** removed their hats as the flag was carried by.

Fido, Jock, and Lacy won the awards for biggest dog, smallest dog, and most beautiful dog, **respectively**.

rise, raise. See *raise, rise*.

sensual, sensuous. *Sensual* means "gratifying the physical appetites" and usually suggests sexuality. *Sensuous* means "appealing to the senses."

The dancer's costume emphasized her **sensual** movements.

The bright colors and sweet fragrances made a visit to the garden a **sensuous** delight.

should of. Nonstandard for *should have*.

sit, set. *Sit* means "to be seated." It is intransitive and therefore has no object. Its principal parts are *sit, sat, sat*. *Set* means "to put or place." It is a transitive verb and therefore requires an object. Its principal parts are *set, set, set*.

Japanese people often **sit** on the floor to eat. He **sat** on the grass. He has always **sat** in the back row of class.

Set these candlesticks on the table. Last night, I **set** my purse on a restaurant chair and then forgot it there. I had **set** some flowers on the table without realizing there was a hole in the vase.

site, cite. See *cite, site*.

somewheres. Nonstandard for *somewhere*.

sort of, kind of. See *kind of, sort of*.

such a. Colloquial when used to mean *a very* (*such a good time*). In formal writing, use *such a* only when it is followed by a clause beginning with *that*.

It was **such a** boring play **that** we left after the first act.

sure. *Sure* is an adjective. The use of *sure* as an adverb meaning *surely* or *certainly* is colloquial and should be avoided in formal writing.

His aim is **sure**.

Our coastal beaches have **surely** [not *sure*] become polluted.

sure and. Nonstandard for *sure to*.

Be **sure to** [not *sure and*] watch for and eliminate wordiness in your papers.

take, bring. See *bring, take*.

terribly. Colloquial when used to mean *very* or *quite*. Avoid that use in formal writing.

The governor is **very** [not *terribly*] popular at the moment.

than, then. *Than* is a word used in comparisons. *Then* indicates time.

> Recycling paper is much more profitable today **than** it was a few years ago.
>
> First turn the printer on; **then** give the print command.

that, which. In formal writing, some writers use *that* to begin essential clauses (not set off with commas) and *which* to begin nonessential clauses (set off with commas). However, today many writers also use *which* to begin some essential clauses. Use the style your instructor finds acceptable. (For information on essential and nonessential clauses, see 16f, page 27.)

their, there, they're. *Their* is a possessive pronoun meaning "belonging to them." *There* means "in that place" or "to that place." Also, *there* is used with forms of *to be* (*is, are, was,* and so on). *They're* is a contraction of *they are*.

> The geese at the park hide **their** eggs under bushes.
>
> My car is **there**.
>
> **There** is a surfing museum in Santa Cruz, California.
>
> **They're** coming to visit us on Sunday.

theirselves. Nonstandard for *themselves*.

to, too, two. *To* is a preposition, *too* is an adverb, and *two* is a number.

> **Two** people aren't coming **to** dinner, so there are **too** many place settings at the table.

toward, towards. Both are acceptable, but *toward* is more common. Be consistent in the form you use within a piece of writing.

try and. Nonstandard when used for *try to*.

> **Try to** [not *try and*] do the right thing.

uninterested, disinterested. See *disinterested, uninterested*.

unique. *Unique* means "being the only one of its kind." It is illogical to use modifiers with that meaning (*very unique, rather unique*). While *unique* is also often used to mean "unusual" (the *most unique* person I know), that use of the word is colloquial and should be avoided in formal writing.

up. Avoid tacking *up* onto verbs unless it is genuinely required to modify the verb's meaning.

> The mystery novel **ended** [not *ended up*] with a surprising twist.
>
> You must **step up** to get from the patio into the kitchen.

use, used to. *Use* means "to make use of." *Used to* means "accustomed to" or "in the habit of."

> I am **used to** very spicy food, but when I cook for others, I **use** much less hot pepper.

way. Colloquial when used to mean "far." Avoid that use in formal writing.

> The airport is **far** [not *way*] across the city from the hotel.

ways. Colloquial when used for *way*, meaning "distance." Avoid that use in formal writing.

> The business has a long **way** [not *ways*] to go before it can be called successful.

weather, whether. As a noun, *weather* refers to atmospheric conditions. *Whether*, as a conjunction, refers to alternatives.

> Good **weather** is predicted for the weekend.
>
> He hasn't decided **whether** to major in music or math.

well, good. See *good, well*.

where. Considered nonstandard or informal when used for *that*. Avoid that use in formal writing.

> I heard **that** [not *where*] property taxes are going up again.

which, that. See *that, which*.

who, which, that. Use *who* to refer to people and *which* to refer to things. *That* can refer to things or to people.

> The intrepid miners **who** [or **that**] rushed to California in 1849 were often disappointed in their quest for gold, **which** usually turned out to be fruitless.

who's, whose. *Who's* is a contraction of *who is* or *who has; whose* means "belonging to whom."

> When the call came into the police station, the officer asked, "**Who's** willing to help a woman **whose** pet snake just escaped?"

would of. Nonstandard for *would have*.

your, you're. *Your* means "belonging to you"; *you're* is a contraction of "you are."

> **You're** going to need a first-aid kit and high boots for **your** camping trip.

This section covers rules that most native speakers of English take for granted but that are useful for speakers of English as a second language (ESL).

29 / Articles with Count and Noncount Nouns

Articles are noun markers—they signal that a noun will follow. The indefinite articles are *a* and *an*. (See "Glossary of Usage," page 41, for when to use *a* and when to use *an*.) The definite article is *the*. An article may immediately precede a noun: **a** smile, **the** reason. Or it may be separated from the noun by modifiers: **a** slight smile, **the** very best reason.

To know whether to use an article with a noun and which article to use, you must recognize count and noncount nouns. (For an overview of nouns, see 1a, page 1.)

Note: There are various other noun markers, including quantity words *(some, several, a lot of)*, numerals *(one, ten, 120)*, demonstrative adjectives *(this, these)*, possessive adjectives *(my, your, our)*, and possessive nouns *(Jaime's, the school's)*.

Count nouns name people, places, things, or ideas that can be counted and made into plurals, such as *teacher, restroom,* and *joke (one teacher, two restrooms, three jokes)*.

Noncount nouns refer to things or ideas that cannot be counted, such as *flour, history,* and *truth*. The box below lists and illustrates common types of noncount nouns.

Common Noncount Nouns

> *Abstractions and emotions:* anger, bravery, health, pride, truth
> *Activities:* baseball, jogging, reading, teaching, travel
> *Foods:* bread, broccoli, chocolate, cheese, flour
> *Gases and vapors:* air, helium, oxygen, smoke, steam
> *Languages and areas of study:* Korean, Spanish, algebra, history, physics
> *Liquids:* blood, gasoline, lemonade, tea, water
> *Materials that come in bulk form:* aluminum, cloth, dust, sand, soap
> *Natural occurrences:* magnetism, moonlight, rain, snow, thunder
> *Other things that cannot be counted:* clothing, furniture, homework, machinery, money, news, transportation, vocabulary, work

The quantity of a noncount noun can be expressed with a word or words called a **qualifier**, such as *some, a lot of, a unit of,* and so on. (In the following two examples, the qualifiers are shown in *italic* type, and the noncount nouns are shown in **boldface** type.)

Please have *some* **patience**.

We need to buy *two bags of* **flour** today.

Some words can be either count or noncount nouns depending on whether they refer to one or more individual items or to something in general.

Certain **cheeses** give some people headaches.

> This sentence refers to individual cheeses; *cheese* in this case is a count noun.

Cheese is made in almost every country where milk is produced.

> This sentence refers to cheese in general; in this case, *cheese* is a noncount noun.

29a Using *a* or *an* with nonspecific singular count nouns

Use *a* or *an* with singular nouns that are nonspecific. A noun is **nonspecific** when the reader doesn't know its specific identity.

A left-hander faces special challenges with right-handed tools.

> The sentence refers to any left-hander, not a specific one.

Today, our cat proudly brought **a** baby bird into the house.

> The reader isn't familiar with the bird. This is the first time it is mentioned.

29b Using *the* with specific nouns

In general, use *the* with all specific nouns—specific singular, plural, and noncount nouns.

Following are conditions that make a noun specific and therefore require the article *the*.

A noun is specific in the following cases:

- When it has already been mentioned once

  Today, our cat proudly brought a baby bird into the house. Luckily, **the** bird was still alive.

  > *The* is used with the second mention of *bird*.

- When it is identified by a word or phrase in the sentence

  The pockets in the boy's pants are often filled with sand and dirt.

  > *Pockets* is identified by the words *in the boy's pants*.

- When its identity is suggested by the general context

  At Willy's Diner last night, **the** service was terrible and **the** food was worse.

  > The reader can conclude that the service and food being discussed were at Willy's Diner.

- When it is unique

  There will be an eclipse of **the** moon tonight.

  > Earth has only one moon.

- When it is preceded by a superlative adjective (*best, biggest, wisest*)

  The best way to store broccoli is to refrigerate it in an open plastic bag.

29c Omitting articles

Omit articles with nonspecific plurals and noncount nouns. Plurals and noncount nouns are nonspecific when they refer to something in general.

> **Pockets** didn't exist until the end of the 1700's.
> **Service** is as important as **food** to a restaurant's success.
> Iris serves her children homemade **lemonade**.

29d Using *the* with proper nouns

Proper nouns name particular people, places, things, or ideas and are always capitalized. Most proper nouns do not require articles; those that do, however, require *the*. Following are general guidelines about when and when not to use *the*.

Do not use *the* for most singular proper nouns, including names of the following:

- **People and animals** (Benjamin Franklin, Fido)
- **Continents, states, cities, streets, and parks** (North America, Illinois, Chicago, First Avenue, Washington Square)
- **Most countries** (France, Mexico, Russia)
- **Individual bodies of water, islands, and mountains** (Lake Erie, Long Island, Mount Everest)

Use *the* for the following types of proper nouns:

- **Plural proper nouns** (the Turners, the United States, the Great Lakes, the Rocky Mountains)
- **Names of large geographic areas, deserts, oceans, seas, and rivers** (the South, the Gobi Desert, the Atlantic Ocean, the Black Sea, the Mississippi River)
- **Names with the format *the _____ of _____*** (the Fourth of July, the People's Republic of China, the University of California)

30 / Subjects and Verbs

30a Avoiding repeated subjects

In English, a particular subject can be used only once in a clause. Don't repeat a subject in the same clause by following a noun with a pronoun.

> **Incorrect:** The *manager he* asked Dmitri to lock up tonight.
> **Correct:** The **manager** asked Dmitri to lock up tonight.
> **Correct:** **He** asked Dmitri to lock up tonight.

Even when the subject and verb are separated by a long word group, the subject cannot be repeated in the same clause.

> **Incorrect:** The *girl* that danced with you *she is* my cousin.
> **Correct:** The **girl** that danced with you **is** my cousin.

30b Including pronoun subjects and linking verbs

Some languages may omit a pronoun as a subject, but in English, every clause other than a command must have a subject. (In a command, the subject *you* is understood: [**You**] Hand in your papers now.)

> **Incorrect:** The Grand Canyon is in Arizona. *Is* 217 miles long.
> **Correct:** The Grand Canyon is in Arizona. **It is** 217 miles long.

Every English clause must also have a verb, even when the meaning of the clause is clear without the verb.

> **Incorrect:** Angelita's piano teacher very patient.
> **Correct:** Angelita's piano teacher **is** very patient.

30c Including *there* and *here* at the beginning of clauses

Some English sentences begin with *there* or *here* plus a linking verb (usually a form of *to be: is, are*, and so on). In such sentences, the verb comes before the subject (see 6d, pages 11–12).

> **There are** masks in every culture on Earth.
> The subject is the plural noun *masks*, so the plural verb *are* is used.
>
> **Here is** your driver's license.
> The subject is the singular noun *license*, so the singular verb *is* is used.

In sentences like the above, remember not to omit *there* or *here*.

> **Incorrect:** *Are* several chickens in the Bensons' yard.
> **Correct:** **There are** several chickens in the Bensons' yard.

30d Not using the progressive tense of certain verbs

The progressive tenses are made up of forms of *be* plus the *-ing* form of the main verb. They express actions or conditions still in progress at a particular time. (See 6a, page 9.)

> George **will be taking** classes this summer.

However, verbs for mental states, the senses, possession, and inclusion are normally not used in the progressive tense.

> **Incorrect:** All during the movie they *were hearing* whispers behind them.
> **Correct:** All during the movie they **heard** whispers behind them.
>
> **Incorrect:** That box *is containing* a surprise for Pedro.
> **Correct:** That box **contains** a surprise for Pedro.

Common verbs not generally used in the progressive tense are listed in the box on the next page.

Common Verbs Not Generally Used in the Progressive

Thoughts, attitudes and desires: agree, believe, imagine, know, like, love, prefer, think, understand, want, wish

Sense perceptions: hear, see, smell, taste

Appearances: appear, seem, look

Possession: belong, have, own, possess

Inclusion: contain, include

30e Using only transitive verbs for the passive voice

Only transitive verbs (see 1c, page 2)—verbs that take direct objects—can have a passive form (see 6b, page 10). Intransitive verbs cannot be used in the passive voice.

Incorrect: If you don't fix those brakes, an accident *may be happened*.

> *Happen* is an intransitive verb—no object is needed to complete its meaning.

Correct: If you don't fix those brakes, an accident **may happen.**

If you aren't sure whether a verb is transitive or intransitive, check your dictionary. Transitive verbs are indicated with an abbreviation such as *tr. v.* or *v. t.* Intransitive verbs are indicated with an abbreviation such as *intr. v.* or *v. i.*

30f Using gerunds and infinitives after verbs

A **gerund** is the *-ing* form of a verb that is used as a noun: For Walter, **eating** is a day-long activity. An **infinitive** is *to* plus the basic form of the verb (see 6a, page 7): **to eat**. The infinitive can function as an adverb, an adjective, or a noun. Some verbs can be followed by only a gerund or only an infinitive; other verbs can be followed by either. Examples are given in the following lists. There are many others; watch for them in your reading.

Verb + gerund (admit + stealing)
Verb + preposition + gerund (apologize + for + yelling)

Some verbs can be followed by a gerund but not by an infinitive. In many cases, there is a preposition (such as *for, in,* or *of*) between the verb and the gerund. Following are some verbs and verb/preposition combinations that can be followed by gerunds but not by infinitives:

admit	deny	look forward to
apologize for	discuss	postpone
appreciate	dislike	practice
approve of	enjoy	suspect of
avoid	feel like	talk about
be used to	finish	thank for
believe in	insist on	think about

Incorrect: He must *avoid to jog* until his knee heals.
Correct: He must **avoid jogging** until his knee heals.

Incorrect: The instructor *apologized for to be* late to class.
Correct: The instructor **apologized for being** late to class.

Verb + infinitive (agree + to leave)

Following are common verbs that can be followed by an infinitive but not by a gerund:

agree	decide	plan
arrange	have	refuse
claim	manage	wait

Incorrect: The children *want going* to the beach.
Correct: The children **want to go** to the beach.

Verb + noun or pronoun + infinitive (cause + them + to flee)

Below are common verbs that are first followed by a noun or pronoun and then by an infinitive (not a gerund):

cause	force	remind
command	persuade	warn

Incorrect: The coach *persuaded Mario studying* harder.
Correct: The coach **persuaded Mario to study** harder.

Following are common verbs that can be followed either by an infinitive alone or by a noun or pronoun and an infinitive:

ask	need	want
expect	promise	would like

Dena **asked to have** a day off next week.
Her boss **asked her to work** on Saturday.

Verb + gerund or infinitive (begin + packing or begin + to pack)

Following are verbs that can be followed by either a gerund or an infinitive:

begin	hate	prefer
continue	love	start

The meaning of each of the above verbs remains the same or almost the same whether a gerund or an infinitive is used.

Faith hates **being** late.

Faith hates **to be** late.

With the verbs below, the gerunds and the infinitives have very different meanings.

forget	remember	stop

Esta **stopped to call** home.
> She interrupted something to call home.

Esta **stopped calling** home.
> She discontinued calling home.

31 / Adjectives

31a Following the order of adjectives in English

Adjectives modify nouns and pronouns. In English, an adjective usually comes directly before the word it describes or after a linking verb, in which case it modifies the subject (see 1c, pages 1–2). In each of the following two sentences, the adjective is **boldfaced** and the noun it describes is *italicized*.

That is a **false** *story*.

The *story* is **false**.

When more than one adjective modifies the same noun, the adjectives are usually stated in a certain order, though there are often exceptions. Following is the typical order of English adjectives:

Typical Order of Adjectives in a Series

> 1. *An article or other noun marker:* a, an, the, Lee's, this, three, your
> 2. *Opinion adjective:* dull, handsome, unfair, useful
> 3. *Size:* big, huge, little, tiny
> 4. *Shape:* long, short, round, square
> 5. *Age:* ancient, medieval, old, new, young
> 6. *Color:* blue, green, scarlet, white
> 7. *Nationality:* Italian, Korean, Mexican, Vietnamese
> 8. *Religion:* Buddhist, Catholic, Jewish, Muslim
> 9. *Material:* cardboard, gold, marble, silk
> 10. *Noun used as an adjective:* house (as in *house call*), tea (as in *tea bag*), wall (as in *wall hanging*)

Here are some examples of the above order:

a long cotton scarf

the beautiful little silver cup

your new lavender evening gown

Ana's sweet Mexican grandmother

In general, use no more than two or three adjectives after the article or other noun marker. Numerous adjectives in a series can be awkward: **the beautiful big new blue cotton** sweater.

31b Using the present and past participles as adjectives

The present participle ends in *-ing*. Past participles of regular verbs end in *-ed* or *-d*; a list of the past participles of many common irregular verbs appears on page 11. Both types of participles may be used as adjectives. A participle used as an adjective may precede the word it describes: It was an **exciting** *ballgame*. It may also follow a linking verb and describe the subject of the sentence: The *ballgame* was **exciting**.

While both present and past participles of a particular verb may be used as adjectives, their meanings differ. Use the present participle to describe whoever or whatever causes a feeling: an **embarrassing** *incident* (the incident is what causes the embarrassment). Use the past participle to describe whoever or whatever experiences the feeling: the **embarrassed** *parents* (the parents are the ones who are embarrassed).

The long day of holiday shopping was **tiring**.

The shoppers were **tired**.

Following are pairs of present and past participles with similar distinctions:

annoying / annoyed	exhausting / exhausted
boring / bored	fascinating / fascinated
confusing / confused	frightening / frightened
depressing / depressed	surprising / surprised
exciting / excited	

32 / Prepositions Used for Time and Place

The use of prepositions in English is often idiomatic, and exceptions to general rules are not rare. Therefore, correct preposition use must be learned gradually through experience. Following is a chart showing how three of the most common prepositions are used in some customary references to time and place:

The Use of *On, In,* and *At* to Refer to Time and Place

> *Time*
>
> ***On*** *a specific day:* on Monday, on January 1, on your anniversary
>
> ***In*** *a part of a day:* in the morning, in the daytime (but *at* night)
>
> ***In*** *a month or a year:* in December, in 1776
>
> ***In*** *a period of time:* in an hour, in a few days, in a while
>
> ***At*** *a specific time:* at 10:00 a.m., at midnight, at sunset, at dinnertime
>
> *Place*
>
> ***On*** *a surface:* on the desk, on the counter, on a ceiling
>
> ***In*** *a place that is enclosed:* in my room, in the office, in the box
>
> ***At*** *a specific location:* at the mall, at his house, at the ballpark

This section provides guidelines for the writing of paragraphs, essays, and research papers.

33 / Writing a Paragraph

While paragraph functions vary, a typical paragraph is a series of sentences about one main idea, or point. Such a paragraph often starts with the main idea, expressed in a topic sentence, and the rest of the paragraph provides specific details to support and develop that idea. Consider the following paragraph written by a student named Paul Watkins.

Spanking

Spanking is a poor way to discipline children. First of all, spanking teaches children the wrong lessons. They learn that physical force is an acceptable way to deal with a problem. Spanking also teaches them that bigger, stronger people are entitled to hit smaller, weaker people. Carla, a single mother, realized this effect of spanking after her four-year-old son smacked her two-year-old for being "bad." Secondly, a spanking often has more to do with a parent's emotions than the child's behavior. Parents whose lives are stressful are more likely to strike a child to ease their own frustrations than to teach the child a lesson. Carla also observed this temptation in herself when she hit her ten-year-old daughter after a frustrating day at work. Finally, spanking is just not the most effective discipline. Children who are taught reasoning and consistent, meaningful standards develop better internal self-control than children who behave only to avoid getting hit. Carla recently decided to give up spanking and take a more reasoning approach. She now feels that her children are taking more responsibility for their own behavior and that her home is a safer place.

The above paragraph starts with the topic sentence: "Spanking is a poor way to discipline children." Watkins then goes on to support his main point with three ideas. The first is that spanking teaches a child the wrong lessons. The second supporting idea is that parents with stressful lives are likely to spank children to make themselves feel better, not to teach the children something. The third supporting point is that spanking doesn't work as well as teaching reasoning and consistent, meaningful standards.

33a Two elements of effective writing

Now that you have considered an effective student paragraph, you can see that there are two elements to a successful piece of writing:

1 A main idea. It is often best to state that idea in the first sentence of your paper, just as Watkins has in his paragraph about spanking. However, the topic sentence may also come after a few sentences of introduction or transition or at the end of a paragraph, or it may even be implied.

2 Support for the main idea. Use **specific support**. The more precise and particular your supporting details are, the better your readers can "see," "hear," and "feel"

them. The support in a paragraph may include examples, reasons, descriptions, and other details that help readers accept the validity of the main idea.

In addition, it is important to use **valid support**— all of the details must actually support the main idea. Resist the temptation to add interesting but irrelevant information to a paragraph. Imagine how it would have weakened the paragraph about spanking if Watkins had decided to inject a few details on how useful violence can be in a football game or a war.

Finally, work to achieve **organized, logically connected support**. The supporting details should be organized in a manner that allows readers to follow your points and reasoning. The main topics of your paper and the relationship between your ideas should be clear. Although ideas can be organized in numerous ways, paragraphs are generally best developed in one or two of a few basic patterns: illustration, description, narration, process, comparison and contrast, definition, classification, and cause and effect.

Another way to help your readers follow your line of thought is to use signal words known as transitions. **Transitions** are words and phrases that indicate the relationships between ideas. For example, Watkins has used a transition to help readers notice each time he introduces a new point: *first of all, secondly,* and *finally*. A few more transitions for introducing new points appear below, along with examples of other types of transitions.

Examples of Transitions

To introduce a list of points: also, another, furthermore, in addition, next, last of all, finally

To illustrate: for example, for instance, including, such as, to illustrate

To compare: as, like, likewise, in the same way, similarly

To contrast: but, in contrast, however, nevertheless, on the contrary

To emphasize: above all, indeed, in fact, in other words, most importantly

To show time: after, before, then, until, when

To show cause and effect: as a result, because, consequently, therefore, thus

Finally, keep your main topics in the reader's mind by repeating key words or variations on them. Note that Watkins has repeated the word *spanking* to make it clear to readers that each of his points is about spanking. He avoids overusing that word (or *spanked* or *to spank*) by using *physical force, hit, smacked,* and *to strike*.

33b Steps to effective writing

Even professional writers do not sit down and automatically, in one draft, write a paper. Instead, they have to work on it a step at a time. Writing is a process that can be divided into five steps. This process is the same whether you're composing a paragraph or a longer piece of writing.

Step 1: Getting started through prewriting

There are several prewriting strategies that will help you do the thinking needed to figure out both the point you want to make and the support you have for that point.

Freewriting is just sitting down and writing whatever comes into your mind about a topic. Do this for ten minutes or so. Write without stopping and without worrying at all about spelling, grammar, or the like. Simply get down on paper all the information about the topic that occurs to you.

Here is a bit of the freewriting done by Paul Watkins. He had been given the assignment "Write about a common family problem." Watkins felt right away that he could write about spanking. He began prewriting as a way to explore and generate details on that topic.

> I see too much spanking in families, at home, in the supermarket, everywhere. Parents seem to spank without thought. The anger that comes out is much greater than the offense, they just whip out their hand and hit and think about it later. May not do them or the kids any good at all.

Questioning is a way of thinking about your topic by writing down a series of questions and answers about it. Here are a couple of questions that Watkins might have asked while developing his paper, as well as some answers to those questions:

> How does spanking discipline children? Makes them fearful of getting caught.

> When is a parent likely to spank? When a child has done something wrong. When the parent is feeling stressed.

In addition to asking *how* and *when* questions, you should also ask *who, what, where,* and *why* questions.

When **clustering**, you begin by stating your subject in a few words in the center of a blank sheet of paper. Then, as ideas come to you, put them in ovals, boxes, or circles around the subject, and draw lines to connect them to the subject. Put minor ideas or details in smaller boxes or circles, and use connecting lines to show how they relate as well.

Keep in mind that there is no right or wrong way of clustering. It is a way to think on paper about how various ideas and details relate to one another. Below is an example of some of the clustering that Watkins might have done to develop his ideas.

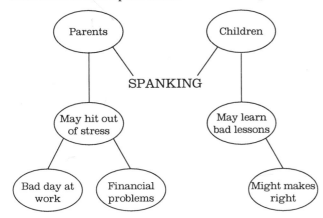

List making, a strategy also known as **brainstorming**, means the listing of ideas and details that could go into your paper. Simply pile these items up, one after another, without worrying about putting them in any special order. Watkins made up a list of details based on some freewriting he had done. Following are a few of those details.

> Spanking may do more harm than good
> Kids may learn wrong lessons
> One is that might makes right
> Woman hits her son, son hits his younger brother
> Parent may spank after a hard day at work

What to expect from prewriting. Some writers may use only one of the prewriting strategies. Others may use bits and pieces of all four of them. Any one strategy can lead to another. Freewriting may lead to questioning or clustering, which may then lead to a list. During this early stage of the writing process, there probably will be a constant moving back and forth as you work to discover your point and just how you will develop it. The goal of prewriting is to get a lot of information down on paper. It's better to spend some time on this stage than to waste time writing a paragraph for which you have no solid point and too little interesting support. You can then add to, shape, and subtract from your raw material as you take your paper through a series of writing drafts.

Keep in mind that prewriting can also help you choose from several topics. Watkins might not have been so sure about which family problem to write about. Then he could have made a list of possible topics—several family problems he could think of. After selecting two or three topics from the list, he could have done some prewriting on each to see which seemed most promising. After finding a likely topic, Watkins would have continued with his prewriting activities until he had a solid main idea and plenty of support.

Step 2: Preparing a scratch outline

A **scratch outline** is a brief plan for the paragraph. It shows at a glance the point of the paragraph and the main support for that point. This rough outline often follows the prewriting stage, or it may gradually emerge in the midst of prewriting. In fact, trying to outline is a good way to see if you need to do more prewriting. If a solid outline does not emerge, then you know you need to do more prewriting to clarify your main point or its support. Once you have a workable outline, you may realize, for instance, that you want to do more list making to develop one of the supporting details in the outline.

As Watkins was working on his list of details, he discovered what the plan of his paragraph could be. He used that list to construct the following scratch outline:

> Spanking is a poor idea
>
> 1. Teaches wrong lessons
> 2. May be done for wrong reason--parent's mood
> 3. Not as effective as reasoning and standards

Once he had an outline as a guide, Watkins was ready to write the first draft of his paper.

Step 3: Writing the first draft

When you do a first draft, be prepared to put in additional thoughts and details that didn't emerge in your prewriting activity. It was while Watkins was writing the first draft that he realized the need to add some details about Carla to illustrate his points. And don't worry if you hit a snag. Just leave a blank space or add a comment such as "Do later" and press on to finish the paper. Also, don't worry yet about grammar, punctuation, or spelling. You don't want to take time correcting words or sentences that you may decide to remove later. Instead, make it your goal to develop the content of your paper with plenty of specific details.

Step 4: Revising

Revising is as much a stage in the writing process as prewriting, outlining, and doing the first draft. **Revising** means that you rewrite a paper, building upon what has been done to make it stronger and better. Look not only for errors, but also for ways to improve your organization and sentences. (See, for example, "Sentence Variety and Style," pages 21–24, and "Word Choice," pages 24–25.) When revising, you write at least one or two more drafts—and perhaps even more drafts of trouble spots.

Step 5: Proofreading

Proofreading, the final step in the writing process, is checking a paper carefully for spelling, grammar, punctuation, and other errors. You are ready for this stage when you are satisfied with your choice of supporting details, the order in which they are presented, and the way they and your topic sentence are worded.

At this point in his work, Watkins used his dictionary to check on the spelling of a couple of words. He used grammar reference materials (such as the "Grammar," "Effective Sentences," "Punctuation," and "Usage" units in this book) to be sure his writing was correct. Watkins also read through the paper carefully, looking for typing errors, omitted words, and any other errors he may have missed before.

Some proofreading tricks can help you see what is really in your paper instead of what you *think* is there. One is to read the paper out loud, noting exactly the words you have written. Another is to take a sheet of paper and cover your writing so that you can expose and carefully check one line at a time. A third strategy is to read your paper backward, from the last sentence to the first. Doing so helps keep you from getting caught up in the flow of the paper and missing small mistakes.

Most instructors will allow you to add several corrections to a paper and still hand it in. Just make the corrections neatly. Add missing punctuation marks right in the text, exactly where they belong. Draw a straight line through any words or punctuation you wish to eliminate or correct. Add new material by inserting a caret (∧) at the point where the addition should be. Then write the new word or words above the line at that point. Retype or recopy a page if you discover a number of errors. If you are using a word processor or computer, make all the corrections in the file and print out a clean copy.

34 / Writing an Essay

An essay does much the same thing a paragraph does: it generally starts with an idea and then provides specific details to support and develop that idea. However, since an essay is much longer than one paragraph, it allows a writer to develop a topic in more detail. Yet the process of writing it is the same as that for writing a paragraph: prewriting, preparing a scratch outline, writing and revising drafts, and proofreading.

Here are the major differences between a paragraph and an essay:

Paragraph	Essay
Includes, usually at the beginning, the main idea of the paragraph, expressed in the **topic sentence**.	Starts with an introductory paragraph containing the central idea of the essay, often expressed in a sentence called the **thesis statement** (or **thesis sentence**).
Body of paragraph made up of sentences that support and develop the topic sentence.	Body of essay made up of paragraphs that support and develop the central idea. Each of these paragraphs has its own main supporting point, stated in a topic sentence.
Paragraph often ends with a closing sentence that rounds it off.	Essay ends with a concluding paragraph that rounds it off.

34a   A sample essay

Later in his writing course, Paul Watkins was asked to expand his paragraph into an essay. Here is the resulting essay:

Children provide their parents with great joy and satisfaction, but they also inspire in parents the most intense anger and frustration. A parent may be faced with a child's maddening, naughty, obnoxious behavior at any hour of the day. Often, the quickest, easiest response to that behavior is a spanking. However, spanking is a poor disciplinary tool. It teaches a dangerous lesson, often stems from the adult's mood, and is an inferior way of changing a child's behavior.

First of all, spanking teaches children to resort to violence. Carla began to realize this on the morning that Gary, her four-year-old, had been a real handful. It was raining, and he was whining because he couldn't go to the park. The tension between Gary and his mother mounted until he squirted most of a new tube of toothpaste into the bathroom sink. Carla swatted his rear end hard, scolding him for being wasteful. Crying, he disappeared into the living room with his two-year-old brother, Zack. A few minutes later Carla heard a squall from Zack. Looking into the living room, she saw the boys surrounded by their crayons and coloring books and Gary paddling Zack's diapered bottom as hard as he could. Gary announced, "I had to spank him, Mom. He broke a crayon. That was really wasteful, wasn't it?" Carla's spanking had taught Gary that hitting is an appropriate response to a problem and that bigger people have the right to use violence against smaller people. Calling it spanking may make it seem OK, but basically that's what it is: a big person hitting a smaller person.

A second important reason not to use spanking is that it often has more to do with releasing an adult's anger than with correcting a child's behavior. Consider the encounter between Ross and his daughter Elsie. Ross had returned home from a terrible day of work that had ended with his accidentally pumping gasoline on his pants and shoes. He entered the house to have Elsie, who was then ten, look up and say, "Can we go out for dinner? Gee, you stink." All Ross's pent-up anger at his boss, coworkers, and the gas pump poured out at her. Snatching up the sneakers that Elsie had kicked off, Ross began smacking Elsie's bottom, yelling about her rudeness, her messiness, and the cost of a restaurant meal. As the astonished child sobbed, "I'm sorry, Daddy! Stop it!" Ross realized that he was furious at the world, but he was hitting his daughter.

Many parents will say, "Spanking is the only thing that really teaches a child a lesson." However, spanking teaches negative lessons, while nonviolent discipline can teach positive lessons. Effective discipline includes strategies like discussion, reasoning, consistent and meaningful standards, and nonviolent punishments like "time-outs" or withdrawal of privileges. It helps a child rethink his or her behavior and consider how to handle a situation better next time. Spanking just hurts. It leaves the child angry, humiliated, and frightened. He or she comes away thinking thoughts of anger, revenge, and avoidance of punishment, not of genuine remorse or increased consideration for others. One young mother, Leona, used to slap her five-year-old's hand when he reached into the cookie jar shortly before dinner. One afternoon she heard him whisper to his little sister, "Don't take a cookie now. Wait 'til Mom's gone." The slapping had taught the boy to avoid his mother's scrutiny, not to stop reaching for cookies before dinner.

Not spanking doesn't mean ignoring misbehavior. Adults don't need physical punishment to learn a positive lesson, and neither do children. In fact, their lesson will be more positive without the negative example of physical force and without a stressed-out adult meting out punishment that is totally out of proportion to the misbehavior. By acting calmly and rationally, a parent can teach a child better behavior through word and through deed.

34b The parts of an essay

When Paul Watkins expanded his paragraph on spanking into an essay, he knew he would need to write an introductory paragraph, several supporting paragraphs, and a concluding paragraph. Each of these parts of the essay is explained below.

1 Introductory paragraph. Use a strategy in the introductory paragraph that will gain your reader's interest, such as one of the following time-tested methods:

a. Begin with a broad statement and narrow it down to your thesis statement. Broad statements can capture your reader's interest while introducing your general topic. They may provide useful background material as well. Watkins could have started his essay by talking about how parents serve as role models. He could then have narrowed that idea down to the point that spanking provides a bad role model.

b. Present an idea or situation that is the opposite of what will be written about. This approach shows the difference between your opening idea or situation and the one to be discussed in the essay. Watkins begins his essay, for example, by showing how spanking is an easy response to a child's misbehavior. That idea contrasts with his main point—that spanking is an inappropriate response.

c. Tell a brief story. In an introduction, a story should be no more than a few sentences, and it should relate meaningfully to—and so lead the reader toward—your central idea. In his introduction, Watkins could have used an anecdote about a parent and a child to show how tempting or how counterproductive spanking can be.

d. Ask one or more questions. The questions may be ones that you intend to answer in your essay, or they may show that your topic relates directly to readers. For instance, Watkins might have started his essay with such questions as *Do your children drive you to distraction?* and *Do you find spanking a handy household tool?*

2 Supporting paragraphs. The main idea of a supporting paragraph is often expressed in a topic sentence. Note that each of the three supporting paragraphs in Watkins's essay has its own topic sentence. The first sentence of each of the first two supporting paragraphs is the topic sentence. In the last supporting paragraph, the second sentence is the topic sentence.

3 Concluding paragraph. An essay that ended with its final supporting paragraph would probably leave the reader wondering if the author is really finished. A concluding paragraph is needed for a sense of completion. As with introductions, there are various common methods of conclusions. Here are two.

a. Provide a summary and a final thought. Using different wording than in your introduction, restate your thesis and main supporting points. This review gives readers an overview of your essay and helps them remember what they've read. Watkins uses this approach in his final paragraph.

b. Focus on the future. A focus on the future often involves a prediction or a recommendation. This method of conclusion may refer in a general way to the central idea, or it may even include a summary. Watkins, for example, might have ended by discussing how improved discipline can change a child's future development.

35 / Writing a Research Paper

Writing a research paper is a longer, more time-consuming project than a paragraph and most essays. It involves the added steps of researching and acknowledging sources, and it demands more careful time management. As soon as a paper is assigned, begin thinking about a topic and map out a tentative schedule for doing prewriting as needed, preparing a working bibliography, taking notes, outlining, writing, revising, and proofreading.

35a Finding a topic to research

Since you will be spending a lot of time and effort on your research paper, take enough time to choose a topic that interests you and that is worth exploring. You will find prewriting techniques helpful in thinking about possible subjects and in whittling down your topic to a manageable size. For example, the topic of punishment would be too broad—it covers every type of punishment, from being kept after school to being executed. A writer interested in punishment could use prewriting to consider instead various narrower topics, such as that of physical punishment.

Once you have your topic, find a question about it that you are interested in, or draft a working thesis statement. As you do so, you may realize that you need to narrow your focus even further. You would probably find, for instance, that a question about the value of physical punishment needs to be trimmed down, perhaps to the value of spanking within the family, the same issue that Paul Watkins discussed in his paragraph and essay. Of course, in a research paper the supporting points for such an issue would have to be developed with information gained from research.

35b Researching

To decide on or confirm your thesis statement and then to find support for it, you'll need to read or skim all or parts of various books and articles. If you find very little information on your subject, you may need to broaden your thesis. If you find an overwhelming amount of material, you may decide to narrow the scope of your work. As your thesis statement becomes sufficiently narrow and firm, you can begin searching for materials likely to provide supporting information.

Searching through the library catalog. Every library has a card catalog that provides the titles and locations of books and other materials. Many libraries have their card catalog on a computer database, which allows users to search quickly for materials by typing in topics, authors, and titles. Follow the directions provided, or ask a librarian for assistance with this and any other part of your search. As you proceed to look for sources in a card catalog, you will discover which key words to use in your search. Two key terms in the search for information on spanking at home, for example, are *corporal punishment* and *child abuse*.

Searching through periodical indexes. Just as a card catalog is an indispensable guide to books on a topic, indexes are a key tool in the search for articles in periodicals (magazines, journals, and newspapers). Some indexes list articles in general magazines and newspapers. These indexes are especially useful as you seek an overview of your subject and work to hone your thesis statement. More specialized indexes are likely to provide added sources of supporting information for your paper.

Indexes may be available in printed volumes or in on-line or CD-ROM databases that are available through a computer terminal. Conducting a search through a database is very similar to searching on a computerized card catalog. In addition to bibliographic information, an abstract (a summary) or sometimes an entire article may be shown on the screen. An abstract can save you time by telling you whether it is worthwhile to read a particular article. At many libraries, the bibliographic information, abstract, and article can be printed out.

If you are using an on-line service such as CompuServe, go to the reference section of the service. Then select the newspaper or magazine database you wish to search. (It's a good idea to read the basic instructions and pricing policies before you begin your search; some on-line services charge for each article displayed or downloaded.) Once in the database, you'll be asked to enter key words for the topic that you are researching. Following the search, you'll be shown a list of the available articles, including their titles, sources, dates of publication, and lengths. At this point, you may select articles from the list and either read them on-screen or print them out for later reading.

When Paul Watkins did such a search on CompuServe for a research paper on corporal punishment, he went to the Magazine Database Plus, selected "QuickSearch," typed the words *corporal punishment*, found twenty-one articles, chose the eleven whose titles seemed most promising, and then printed out the articles. He also accessed the Health and Fitness magazine database, found thirty-four articles, and printed out ten of them. In little more than half an hour, he had twenty-one articles to consider using for his paper!

Building a working bibliography. As you conduct your library search, prepare a bibliography of sources that are likely to be useful in writing your paper. Write your record for each source on an index card. The card should include information you need to find the reference, including the call numbers of books. To make it easier to prepare the list of references you'll eventually need at the end of your paper, write out complete bibliographic information on the card in the style your instructor asks you to use. (If you are asked to use the Modern Language Association [MLA] style of documentation, see "MLA Style," pages 59–64. If you are asked to use the American Psychological Association [APA] style, see "APA Style," pages 65–68.) Later, if you have used a particular reference in writing your paper, you will already have the necessary entry for your list of sources.

Bibliography Cards for an MLA-Style Paper

Straus, Murray A. Beating the Devil Out of Them:
Corporal Punishment in American Families. New
York: Macmillan, 1994.
HQ770.4.S77 1994

Samalin, Nancy. "What's Wrong with Spanking?"
Parents Magazine July 1992: 56–59. Magazine
Database Plus. On-line. CompuServe. 13 Apr. 1995.

To avoid accumulating an overly long working bibliography, evaluate carefully the references you consider. Stick to information that may answer the question you are writing about or that may support your thesis statement. On the other hand, it is better to include resources you're not sure about. It is easier to record information about a reference than to find a book or article that you have changed your mind about but have lost track of.

If you are working at a library where it is possible to print out the bibliographic information, you may wish to work from the printouts when preparing your list of sources.

Using other sources. In addition to books and periodicals, consider other useful resources at the library, such as pamphlets, films, videos, records, and audio tapes. Businesses and professional associations are also possible sources of information. Make any requests for literature from such organizations early in your search, keeping in mind that it may not come for several weeks (or even in time for you to use). And check with your librarian before you request the information; it may already be available in the library.

Finally, you may wish to interview experts for information to include in your paper or for advice on how to proceed. If you arrange such an interview, be sure you are well prepared with questions that will draw out the information you are after. You will need to have already done some reading on your topic to prepare useful questions. Since interviewers rarely remember as much as they think they will, take careful notes dur-

ing the interview, or use a tape recorder if the person you interview permits. After, send the person you interviewed a short thank-you note, a basic courtesy to someone who has taken time to assist you.

35c Taking notes

Much of the work on your paper will be in the form of carefully written notes. As you take notes on a particular source, you will need to make decisions about which material you wish to quote, which points you wish to restate in your own words, and which sections you wish to summarize. To avoid plagiarism, use quotation marks for all quoted material, and copy the material carefully, including punctuation and capitalization. When paraphrasing, reword a point entirely in your own words; changing a few of the author's words is not sufficient to avoid plagiarism. Finally, don't forget to credit the source of every piece of information.

To avoid wasting much time on reading sources and taking notes that won't contribute to your paper, take a few moments to evaluate how useful a reference will be. Use tables of contents and indexes to zero in quickly on relevant parts of a book. Read the beginning of an article or chapter and perhaps skim the rest of the piece. Don't get sidetracked by interesting materials that don't relate to your question or thesis statement, and avoid articles that are out of date.

You will find it helpful to take notes on index cards, writing information from only one source and on only one subject per card. Write the subject at the top of the card so you can see it at a glance. The cards, easily rearranged, will make it easy for you to experiment later with the organization of your paper. Using index cards will also make it easy for you to eliminate any notes you eventually decide are not useful.

In addition to your notes, carefully record on each card the author's last name and the exact page(s) where the information was found. If the author has written more than one work in your bibliography, also include a shortened form of the title. Then later you will be in no doubt about which bibliographic citation to include in your list of sources.

Note Card with Summary and Quotation

Making spanking illegal	*Straus, Beating,*
	161–162
Since spanking is so common, many believe that it is	
impractical to expect parents not to spank their chil-	
dren. However, just because something is done	
doesn't mean that it should be legal. "It is no more	
unrealistic to expect parents to never hit a child than	
to expect that husbands should never hit their wives."	

To differentiate between the cards you use for notes and those you've used for your working bibliography, you may wish to use different-sized cards, two colors of cards, or two colors of ink.

You may occasionally want to save time by photo-copying material from a book or article. If so, take a few moments to indicate on the photocopy which material you plan to quote, summarize, and paraphrase. Later, when you have more time, you may wish to transfer the important information to note cards.

35d Reconsidering your thesis statement and preparing an outline

Once you have done your research, reexamine your thesis statement. Do you think it will work as is, or based on what you now know, does it need reformulating? Once you are satisfied with it, begin planning the order of your paper. Prepare a scratch outline of all the main points you can think of that you'd like to use in support of your thesis statement. Once you've decided on those points and their order, begin to insert details where they belong under the main points. Keep revising your outline until you feel it will be a good guide to writing the first draft of your paper. (If your instructor asks for an outline of your paper, this working outline will serve as a good starting point.)

35e Drafting, revising, and proofreading the research paper

Writing and proofing the research paper is much like writing and proofing a paragraph and an essay (see "Writing a Paragraph," pages 52–54, and "Writing an Essay," pages 54–55). One important difference, however, is the need to credit your sources using the style requested by your instructor. The unit on "Documentation" on pages 59–68 explains how to prepare in-text citations in the MLA and APA styles.

Keep in mind that in working on a paper, you can go back and forth between stages as necessary. As you write your paper, be prepared to make adjustments in your outline or even to go back and get a few more research notes to fill in a gap.

Following are the first two pages of a research paper that Paul Watkins prepared on spanking.

Sample Pages of a Research Paper: MLA Format

Watkins 1

Paul Watkins

Professor Josephs

English 101

12 May 1995

Corporal Punishment: The Unintended Effects

Natalie Owens was watching Oprah Winfrey and preparing dinner while Lucas, age five, and Doug, three, played quietly in the back yard. Suddenly, a blood-curdling scream jolted her attention. On her flight to the back door, she glanced out the window to see Lucas whacking Doug with a metal shovel from the sandbox. Outside in seconds, Owens responded as she felt any good mother should—she spanked Lucas soundly. And to be sure he got the point, she barked, "That will teach you to use force!" (Owens). Like Owens at that time, most Americans approve of physical discipline (Stark), and most parents use it at least occasionally from the time their children are infants until they are teens (Straus, Beating 21). Yet research shows that such punishment has far-reaching negative effects. Children who are hit are more likely, among other things[1], to commit crimes, to suffer from depression and thoughts of suicide,and to be violent in their personal lives.

Watkins 2

First of all, children who are physically punished are more likely to participate in various acts of delinquency. In the second National Family Violence Survey, social scientist Murray A. Straus, founder and co-director of the Family Research Lab at the University of New Hampshire, and colleagues studied the effects of corporal punishment on young people. Straus explains the general design and finding of this study:

> We focused on children aged eight through seventeen. . . . The survey contained data that could be used to control for the overlap of spanking with several family characteristics that might be the real cause of a relationship between spanking and these crimes. These included whether the parents were violent to each other, whether there was a drinking problem, and whether they were otherwise competent parents, as well as other family characteristics that are related to delinquency. We found that, even after controlling for the overlap between corporal punishment and other family characteristics, corporal punishment by itself is related to delinquency. (Beating 109).

36 / An Overview of Documentation

Research papers as well as many reports and articles require documentation of all facts, opinions, and quotations taken from other sources. Sources are generally documented in two ways: 1) as citations within the text and 2) in a list of sources at the end of the text.

36a Citations within the text

Include citations within the text of your paper for all quotations as well as for paraphrases and summaries of facts and opinions obtained from your research. By acknowledging sources of borrowed information, writers give fair credit and avoid plagiarism. For instance, read the comment below on E. E. Cummings's poetry by Louis Untermeyer in the book *Modern American Poetry: A Critical Anthology*.

His preoccupation with typographical design has often tricked him; much of his work suffers because of his distortions and that part of it which succeeds is successful in spite of, and not because of, its form.

Below are two ways of reporting on the above comment.

Any successes in Cummings's poetry come not from the unusual typographical designs, but despite them.

Untermeyer feels that any successes in Cummings's poetry come not from the unusual typographical designs, but despite them (567).

The first report above plagiarizes Untermeyer's work. The second properly credits Untermeyer for the observation. (The number in parentheses is the relevant page number, in accordance with the MLA style.)

Citation styles vary, but each includes enough detail about a reference so that your reader can find it in a list of sources at the end of the paper.

36b List of sources

A list at the end of a paper provides key information about all the sources cited within the paper. The Modern Language Association (MLA) calls this list "works cited." The American Psychological Association (APA) calls the list "references."

To cite books, you will usually find the source information you need on the title page and its reverse side, the copyright page. To cite articles in periodicals (such as journals and newspapers), look at the periodical cover, its contents page, and the first page of the article.

36c Styles of documentation

There are various styles of documentation. Use the one your instructor suggests, and always stick to one style in a paper. In general, English and humanities papers use the MLA style, and social science papers use the APA style. These two styles and an alternate MLA style for documentation with footnotes or endnotes are described in the following chapters. If you have any questions not answered here, consult one of the following manuals:

Gibaldi, Joseph. *MLA Handbook for Writers of Research Papers*. 4th ed. New York: MLA, 1995.

American Psychological Association. *Publication Manual of the American Psychological Association*. 4th ed. Washington: American Psychological Assn., 1995.

37 / MLA Style

37a MLA style for citations within the text

In-text citations in the MLA style refer readers to a list of sources (titled "Works Cited") at the end of the paper. In general, each citation includes at least the author's last name and a page number. The basic style is illustrated below for a work by one author, followed by examples of other types of in-text citations in the MLA style.

Work by one author. Give the author's name and the relevant page number. If you do not use the author's name in a sentence, put both the last name and the page number within parentheses with no punctuation between them.

Several studies have found that parents hit girls less often than they hit boys (Straus 29).

If the author's name is in the sentence, put only the page number within the parentheses.

Straus writes, "It is no more unrealistic to expect parents to never hit a child than to expect that husbands should never hit their wives" (161).

No page number is necessary if the source is only one page long.

If a quotation takes more than four typed lines, begin it on a new line and indent an inch (or, on a typewriter, ten spaces), and double-space throughout. If you quote one paragraph or part of one, do not indent the quoted paragraph. If you quote more than one paragraph, indent the second one a quarter inch (or three typewriter spaces) from the quotation's margin. In that case, indent the first paragraph only if it begins with the first sentence of the paragraph.

Quotations set off in this manner are usually introduced with a colon. After the final punctuation mark of the quotation, type one space and insert the parenthetical citation.

Stark reveals the extent of public support for physical punishment both at home and in school:

A full 86 percent of adults say it's all right for parents to hit, spank or physically discipline children, a 1988 Harris poll found. But fewer than half (44 percent) think teachers have that right.

Over half (56 percent) of public school teachers, on the other hand, approve of school spanking, according to a 1989 Gallup poll. (10)

An entire work. To cite an entire work, use only the author's or editor's name in a sentence (which is preferable) or within parentheses:

> Straus makes a strong case against all forms of physical punishment in American families.

> There have been numerous revealing studies on spanking (Straus).

Authors with the same last name. If your sources include books by two or more authors with the same last name, include the first initial in each citation: (M. Straus 29). If the initial is also shared, use the entire first name: (Murray Straus 34–35).

Work by two or more authors. For works by two or three authors, put all the authors' last names in a sentence or within parentheses with the page number: (Kadushin and Martin 20).

For works by four or more authors, you may use all of the authors' names or only the name of the first author followed by *et al.,* the abbreviation for a Latin term meaning "and others": (Dohrenwend et al. 206). Follow the form you use in your list of works cited.

Two or more works by the same author. If one person authored two or more of your cited works, include within the parentheses the full title (if brief) or a shortened form of the title before the page number. Book titles should be underlined: (Beating 161). (Beating is a shortened version of the book title *Beating the Devil Out of Them.*) Article titles should be placed within quotation marks: ("Family Patterns" 460). ("Family Patterns" is a shortened version of the article title "Family Patterns and Child Abuse in a Nationally Representative American Sample.")

If the author's name is not mentioned in your text, put it within the parentheses with the title or abbreviated title, and separate the two with a comma: (Straus, Beating 161).

Work by corporate (group) author. When the "author" of a source is a corporation or other organization, use the organization's name, shortened or in full in the text or within parentheses: (National Center on Child Abuse and Neglect 2).

No author given. When the author's name is unknown, use the full title (if brief) or a shortened version of the title: ("Spanking May Foster Aggression" 1995). (The full title of the article is "Spanking May Foster Aggression Toward Peers in Young Children.")

If you use a shortened version, begin with the first word of the title (other than *a, an,* or *the*) so that your reader can find it in alphabetical order in your list of works cited.

Work in an anthology. Use the name of the author of the work you are citing, not the name of the editor of the book.

Multivolume work. If your list of works cited includes more than one volume of a multivolume work, indicate within the parentheses which volume you are referring to. Follow the volume number by a colon and then the page number: (Hetherington 4:1).

Literary work. Literary citations must include information to help readers refer to a specific edition of a novel, play or poem. For novels, follow the page number with a semicolon and then the part, section, or chapter, using appropriate abbreviations: (4; ch. 1), (130; pt. 1, ch. 1).

For plays and poems, omit page numbers. For a play, list act, scene, and line numbers (if any) separated by periods: (2.1.10–12). Use Arabic numerals for acts and scenes unless your instructor recommends that you use Roman numerals. For a poem, give the number of the part (if there is more than one) and the line numbers; separate the two references with a period: (3.3–4).

> In Hamlet's response to his mother about the appearance of grief, Shakespeare raises the issue of appearances versus reality (1.2.76-86).

> Emily Dickinson also reveals a religious view of nature in "Indian Summer": "Oh, sacrament of summer days / Oh last communion in the haze" (5:1-2).

Indirect source. It is generally best to use material from its original source. However, at times, only a secondhand source is available. When you use a quotation that you found in a work written by somebody else, put *qtd. in* (for "quoted in") before the name of the work's author within the parentheses: (qtd. in Straus 69).

MLA optional information notes with parenthetical documentation

In the MLA style of parenthetical documentation, you may also use notes for two types of information: 1) points that don't fit in your text but that you feel are important enough to include, and 2) information relating to your sources—lengthy citations that you feel may overly interrupt the flow of your text or comments on your sources.

MLA information notes can be either endnotes, which are listed on a separate page or pages just before the list of works cited, or footnotes, which appear at the bottom of the page. The two types of notes are identical except for their location and spacing—endnotes are double-spaced, and footnotes are single-spaced. Unless instructed otherwise, use endnotes; they are generally easier to handle. In either case, insert a superscript (raised) Arabic numeral at each relevant point in the text to correspond to the number of each note. Number the notes consecutively throughout the paper.

Text

> Children who are hit are more likely, among other things[1], to commit crimes, to suffer from depression and thoughts of suicide, and to be violent in their personal lives.

Endnote with comment

1 For a discussion of the points that hitting children even increases the likelihood of their sexuality being associated with imaginary or actual masochistic activities and reduces their future income, see Beating the Devil Out of Them 130-136, 137-146.

For endnotes, begin on a separate page, and center the title *Notes* an inch from the top. Number all pages of the endnotes consecutively, beginning with the number after the last page of the text of your paper, one-half inch from the top and flush with the margin on the right. Double-space between the title and the first note. Indent each note a half inch (or five spaces on the typewriter), beginning with the superscript number. After the number, type one space and begin the reference. Begin any subsequent lines of a note at the left margin.

Footnotes begin four single spaces below the text. They are single-spaced, with double-spacing between them.

(Do not confuse these optional notes with notes that are used as an alternative method of documentation. See 37c, page 64.)

37b MLA list of works cited

Begin the list of citations on a separate sheet of paper with the title *Works Cited* centered an inch from the top of the paper. Number each page of *Works Cited* consecutively, beginning with the number immediately after the last page of the text of your paper (or after a page of informational endnotes, if any). Type your last name and the page number in the upper right-hand corner flush with the right margin and half an inch from the top. Double-space throughout, including between the title and the first citation.

Begin each citation flush with the left margin. If a citation exceeds one line, indent the second and subsequent lines one-half inch (or, if using a typewriter, five spaces).

Alphabetize the entries by the last name of the author or editor (or of the first author or editor). If no author or editor is given for a work, use the first word of the title other than *a*, *an*, or *the*.

A sample "Works Cited" list is on page 64. Following are models of various types of citations for an MLA-style documentation list.

Books and other nonperiodicals. In general, there are three main parts to MLA book citations:

1. The author's name as given on the title page (last name first). Omit titles and degrees before or after a name.

2. The title and any subtitle (underlined). Titles of articles should be put within quotation marks.

3. Publication information: city of publication, publisher, and date of publication. If the book lists several cities, use only the first. Add an abbreviation of the country (or province, for Canada) for cities outside of the United States that may be unfamiliar to readers.

Use a shortened version of a publisher's name, using standard abbreviations where applicable.

The basic format is illustrated below with a book by one author, followed by examples of other types of book entries.

Book by one author

Morrison, Toni. Beloved. New York: Knopf, 1987.

Book by two or more authors

Peters, Tom, and Nancy Austin. A Passion for Excellence. New York: Random, 1985.

(Note that only the first author's name is reversed.)

For a book with four or more authors, you may use the above format, or you may use only the first author's name followed by *et al.*:

Bracey, Hyler, et al. Managing From the Heart. New York: Delacorte, 1990.

Two or more books by the same author

Kozol, Jonathan. Amazing Grace: The Lives of Children and the Conscience of a Nation. New York: Crown, 1995.

- - -. Savage Inequalities: Children in America's Schools. New York: Crown, 1991.

(For the second and subsequent listings by an author or editor, type three hyphens in place of the name, and alphabetize according to the first word of the title other than *a*, *an*, or *the*.)

Book by corporate (group) author

Rand McNally & Company. The Magnificent Continent. Chicago: Rand McNally, 1975.

Anthology

Allen, Donald M., and Robert Creeley, eds. New American Story. New York: Grove, 1965.

Edition of an author's work prepared by an editor

Fitzgerald, F. Scott. The Price Was High: The Last Uncollected Stories of F. Scott Fitzgerald. Ed. Matthew J. Bruccoli. New York: Harcourt, 1979.

(If you are citing the editor's work, begin with the editor's name, followed by a comma and the abbreviation *ed.*, and put the author's name after the title: *By F. Scott Fitzgerald.*)

Book with no author or editor given

The Inventive Yankee: From Rockets to Roller Skates, 200 Years of Yankee Inventors and Inventions. Dublin: Yankee, 1989.

Translation

Raoul Wallenberg. Letters and Dispatches 1924-1944. Trans. Kjersti Board. New York: Arcade, 1995.

(If you are citing the translator's comments, begin with the translator's name, followed by a comma and the abbreviation *trans.*)

Second or later edition

Kaplan, Harriet, Scott J. Bally, and Carol Garretson.

Speechreading: A Way to Improve Understanding.

2nd ed. Washington: Gallaudet UP, 1987.

(*UP* stands for "University Press.")

Multivolume work

Gänzl, Kurt. The Encyclopedia of the Musical Theatre.

Vol. 2. New York: Schirmer, 1994.

(If you are using more than one volume of a multivolume work, cite the total number of volumes: *2 vols.*)

Work in an anthology

Allen, Edward. "River of Toys." The Best American Short

Stories 1990. Ed. Richard Ford with Shannon

Ravenel. Boston: Houghton, 1990. 1-11.

Article in a reference book

Smylie, James H. "Faith Healing." The Encyclopedia

Americana. 1994 ed.

(The abbreviation *ed.* stands for "edition.")

Introduction, foreword, or afterword

Fromm, Erich. Foreword. Summerhill: A Radical

Approach to Child Rearing. By A. S. Neill.

New York: Hart, 1960. ix-xvi.

Brochure or pamphlet

Smithsonian Institution. After the Revolution: Everyday

Life in America 1780-1800. Washington:

Smithsonian, 1985.

Government publication

Department of Justice Immigration and Naturalization

Service. Our Constitution and Government.

Washington: GPO, 1978.

(*GPO* stands for "Government Printing Office," which publishes most federal publications.)

Unpublished dissertation

Gonzalez, Antonio M. "The Hispanic Patient: Clinical

Issues, Ethical Concerns and Implications for

Professional Practice in Mental Health." Diss.

Widener U, 1993.

Published dissertation

Goldstein, Martin E. American Policy Toward Laos.

Diss. U of Pennsylvania, 1968. Rutherford:

Fairleigh Dickinson UP, 1973.

Dissertation abstract

Stitt, Muriel. "Post-Traumatic Stress Disorder and

Battered Women." Diss. Fordham U, 1993.

DAI 54 (1993): 2225B.

(*DAI* stands for *Dissertation Abstracts International*.)

Periodicals. In general, there are three main parts to MLA citations for articles in periodicals:

1. The author's name (last name first). If more than one author is listed, the second and subsequent names are given with the first name first and with no comma between the first and last names.

2. The title of the article (in quotation marks).

3. Publication information: the periodical title (underlined), volume number (for scholarly journals), date of publication, and inclusive page numbers (first through last). When the date of publication includes a month (needed for magazines and newspapers), abbreviate the month, using the first three letters followed by a period, except for *May, June*, and *July*, which are written out.

Following are models of periodical citations in the MLA style.

Article in a journal with continuous pagination from issue to issue in an annual volume

Weiss, Thomas G. "The United Nations at Fifty: Recent

Lessons." Current History 94 (1995): 223-28.

(The volume number is 94. Also note that in MLA style, the second page number is written as 28, not 228.)

Article in a journal with separate pagination for each issue

Klamer, Keith. "Minority Leader." Vocational Education

Journal 70.5 (1995): 36+.

(The citation refers to volume 70, issue 5. The plus sign indicates that the article is not printed on consecutive pages.)

Article in a magazine

Weekly

Begley, Sharon. "Gray Matters." Newsweek 27 Mar.

1995: 48-54.

Monthly

Schwartz, D. M. "All Together, Now: Read Aloud to the

Kids!" Smithsonian Feb. 1995: 82+.

(For magazines, no volume or issue numbers are included in the citation.)

Article in a newspaper

Ziegler, Bart. "In Cyberspace the Web Delivers Junk

Mail." Wall Street Journal 13 June 1995, eastern

ed.: B1+.

(*B1* tells us that the article is in section B beginning on page 1.)

Unsigned article in a newsletter

"Gene Therapy: A Bold New Era in Medicine." The

University of Texas-Houston Health Science Center

Lifetime Health Letter June 1995: 4-5.

Unsigned editorial

"False Promise." Editorial. Philadelphia Inquirer 5 June

1995, South Jersey ed.: A8.

Letter to the editor

Brady, Marion. Letter. Utne Reader Mar.-Apr. 1994: 6-7.

Review

Jackson, Donald Dale. Rev. of The Story of Webster's Third, by Herbert C. Morton. Smithsonian Dec. 1994: 146-47.

Other sources. Following are model citations for several other types of sources. Begin your citation with the name or title being cited—if your paper focuses on the work, put the title first; if your paper cites the director, put that name first; and so on.

Television interview

Diller, Barry. Interview with Ted Koppel. Nightline. ABC. 14 June 1995.

Film

Huston, John, dir., scriptwriter. The Treasure of the Sierra Madre. Warner Bros., 1947.

(If you are not citing the work of an individual, begin with the title, followed by the director, distributor, and year.)

Videocassette

A Time for Justice: America's Civil Rights Movement. Prod. Charles Guggenheim. Videocassette. Teaching Tolerance, 1992.

(Instead of *videocassette*, use the word(s) *videodisc, slide program,* or *filmstrip* when appropriate.)

Sound recording

Taylor, James. "Copperline." New Moon Shine. Columbia, 1991.

(The above recording is on a compact disc. If a cited recording is on any other medium, indicate the medium— *Audiocassette, Audiotape* [reel-to-reel tape], or *LP*—before the manufacturer's name. Follow the medium with a period.)

Live performance of a play

Bad Girls Upset by the Truth. By Jo Carol Pierce. Dir. Ben Levit. Perf. Jo Carol Pierce. Plays and Players Theatre, Philadelphia. 4 June 1995.

Material from an on-line database

From a computer service: material available also in print

Minsky, Marvin. "Will Robots Inherit the Earth?" Scientific American 271.4 (1994): 108-13. Scientific American Online. On-line. America Online. 28 June 1995.

(In a citation for an electronic source also available in print, provide the author's name if available, the same publication information that you would include if the entry were for only the printed source [including the title and print date], the database title [underlined], the medium of publication [*On-line*], the name of the computer service, and the date the material was accessed.)

From a computer service: material available only on-line

National Research Council Committee on Virtual Reality Research and Development. "Technology Gap Exists Between What Is Virtual and What Is Reality." 14 Nov. 1994. NAS Online. On-line. America Online. 28 June 1995.

(In a citation for an electronic source that is available only on-line, provide the author's name [if given], the title [in quotation marks], the date the material was "published" on-line [if given], the database title [underlined], the medium of publication [*On-line*], the name of the computer service, and the date the material was accessed.)

From a computer network: electronic journals, newsletters, conferences

Koehn, Daryl. "The Ethics of Handwriting Analysis in Pre-Employment Screening." The On-Line Journal of Ethics 1 (1995): 34 pars. On-line. Internet. 23 Oct. 1995. Available http://condor.depaul.edu/ ethics/hand.html

(In a citation for an electronic journal, newsletter, or conference, provide the author's name [if given]; the article or document title [in quotation marks]; the journal, newsletter, or conference title [underlined]; the volume, issue, or other identifying number [if given]; the year or date of publication [in parentheses]; the number of paragraphs or pages, after a colon [abbreviated *par., pars., p.* or *pp.* if given, or use *n. pag.* for "no pagination"]; the medium of publication [*On-line*]; the name of the computer service; and the date the material was accessed.

You may also add the electronic address used to access the information. [Some instructors may require it.] That address should be preceded by the word *Available*.)

Computer software

"Anger." The New Grolier Multimedia Encyclopedia. CD-ROM. Danbury: Grolier, 1993.

(If the article is signed, begin with the author's last name, followed by a comma, and then the first name of the author, followed by a period.)

Letter or E-mail communication

Clark, Michael. E-mail to the author. 10 Jan. 1996.

(For a letter you have received, use the wording *letter to the author*.)

Personal interview

Ginsberg, Allen. Telephone interview. 26 Nov. 1995.

(For an in-person interview, use *personal interview* instead of *telephone interview*.)

Sample Works Cited List: MLA Format

Watkins 11

Works Cited

Agnew, Robert. "Physical Punishment and Delinquency." Youth & Society 15 (1983): 225-36.

Harris, Judith Rich, and Robert Liebert. The Child: Development Through Birth to Adolescence. 2d ed. New York: Prentice Hall, 1987.

Owens, Natalie. Personal interview. 1 Apr. 1995.

Samalin, Nancy. "What's Wrong with Spanking?" Parents Magazine July 1992: 56-59. Magazine Database Plus. On-line. CompuServe. 13 Apr. 1995.

"Spanking May Foster Aggression Toward Peers in Young Children." The Menninger Letter Mar. 1995: 1-2.

Stark, Elizabeth. "Spare the Rod in Schools, But Not at Home." Psychology Today Dec. 1989: 10.

Straus, Murray A. Beating the Devil Out of Them: Corporal Punishment in American Families. New York: Macmillan, 1994.

- - -. "Children as Witness to Marital Violence: A Risk Factor for Life-Long Problems Among a Nationally Representative Sample of American Men and Women." Children and Violence: Report of the Twenty-Third Ross Roundtable on Critical Approaches to Common Pediatric Problems. Ed. D. F. Schwartz. Columbus: Ross Laboratories, 1992. 98-109.

- - -. "Sociological Research and Social Policy: The Case of Family Violence." Sociological Forum 7 (1992): 211-37.

37c MLA documentation style using endnotes or footnotes

An alternate documentation style that your instructor may prefer is the MLA style for endnotes or footnotes. This style is used by some scholars in history, religion, theology, and the arts. Both types of notes are identical except for their location. Endnotes are listed together at the end of a paper. Footnotes are placed at the bottom of the page that contains the information being documented. They begin four single-spaced lines below the text and should be single-spaced, with double-spaces between them. Unless instructed to use footnotes, use endnotes, which are easier to handle.

For either, a superscript (raised) Arabic numeral is placed after the point in the text being documented. For smooth reading, place the number at the end of a phrase, clause, or sentence. The same number is placed before the corresponding endnote or footnote, followed by a space. Number the notes consecutively throughout the paper.

Text

According to the Vanderbilt University study, if one parent is hostile and the other is not, the effect of the aggressive parent is counterbalanced by that of the nonaggressive parent.[7]

Endnote

[7] "Spanking May Foster Aggression Toward Peers in Young Children," The Menninger Letter Mar. 1995: 2.

To prepare a page of endnotes, begin on a new page. Number the pages consecutively, beginning with the number that follows the last page of the paper's text. Center the word *Notes* one inch from the top, double-space, and begin the first note. Indent each note one-half inch (or five typewriter spaces). Type the note number as a superscript (raised), type a space, and then type the reference. Begin any second and subsequent lines flush with the left margin. List the notes consecutively, and double-space throughout.

MLA-style note form. The first note for a source provides more or less the same information as an entry in a list of sources. The differences are explained and illustrated below.

A documentation note has four main parts:

1. The author's name (first name first).

2. The title (in quotation marks or underlined, as appropriate).

3. Publication information (in parentheses). (For information on the wording of locations and publishers, see the explanations for the MLA list of works cited in 37b on pages 61 and 62.)

4. The number or numbers of the pages of the specific portion of the work that you refer to, if applicable.

Commas, not periods, are used between the elements of the note. The only period comes at the end of the documentation note.

Shown below are models for a book and a periodical.

[1] Toni Morrison, Beloved (New York: Knopf, 1987) 3-19.

[2] Sharon Begley, "Gray Matters," Newsweek 27 Mar. 1995: 48-54.

Subsequent references. Once a source has been documented fully in a footnote or endnote, subsequent references should include only as much information as is needed to identify the source. Generally, the author's last name and a page number are sufficient. When the author is unknown, use a shortened version of the title.

[5] Wallenberg 52.

[10] The Inventive Yankee 75.

If you cite two or more works by one author, include a shortened version of the title in the citation, either underlining it or placing it within quotation marks as appropriate.

[8] Kozol, Savage Inequalities 20-25.

List of sources. Since the endnotes or footnotes fully document your sources, you may not be asked to include an alphabetized list of your sources. However, if your instructor asks you to include such a list, title the list *Works Cited*. Alternately, your instructor may ask you to include in your list all the sources you consulted in working on your paper, even those not cited in the text. In that case, title the list *Bibliography*. In either case, use the entry formats shown in 37b, pages 61–63.

38 / APA Style

38a APA style for citations within the text

In-text citations in the APA style refer readers to a list of sources (titled "References") at the end of the paper. In general, each citation includes at least the author's last name and the date of publication. The basic style is illustrated below for a work by one author, followed by examples of other types of in-text citations in the APA style.

Work by one author. For a paraphrase or summary of a point, as well as for a reference to an entire work, the citation should include only the author's last name and the date. If the name does not appear in a sentence, put it and the date within parentheses, separated by a comma.

> Several studies have found that parents hit girls less
>
> often than they hit boys (Straus, 1994).

If the author's name is mentioned in the sentence, follow it immediately with the date within parentheses.

> Stark (1989) reports that while men are somewhat more
>
> likely to have been physically punished when young,
>
> women are more likely to do the spanking.

For a quotation, the citation must also include the page number. Insert the number within parentheses at the end of the quotation, even in mid-sentence. Use the abbreviations *p.* for *page* and *pp.* for *pages*.

> Straus (1994) writes, "It is no more unrealistic to expect
>
> parents to never hit a child than to expect that husbands
>
> should never hit their wives" (p. 161).

In the APA style, a quotation of more than forty words should begin on a separate line, be indented five to seven spaces (or as much as an indent for a new paragraph), and be double-spaced. Do not use quotation marks. Do not indent the first line of the quotation for the beginning of a paragraph. If the quotation runs to two or more paragraphs, indent the first line of the second and subsequent paragraphs five to seven spaces from the quotation's margin. Follow the final punctuation of the quotation with one space, and then put the citation within parentheses.

> Hyman (1990) explains that physical punishment in
>
> school can lead to family stress:
>
> > When angry parents confront the school authorities,
> >
> > the bureaucrats almost always support the action of
> >
> > the person who administered the punishment. They
> >
> > may institute a mild penalty such as a written
> >
> > reprimand, but in most cases the disciplinary
> >
> > practices are considered appropriate. The school
> >
> > authorities then begin to question the motives
> >
> > behind the parents' complaints. The parents,
> >
> > especially the mothers, tend to become fearful,
> >
> > depressed, and anxious for their children. (pp. 75-76)

For the second and subsequent references to a work within a paragraph, you may exclude the date if the work won't be confused with another cited in the paper.

Authors with the same last name. If your sources include books by two or more authors with the same last name, include in each citation the author's initials, even if the dates differ: (M. Straus, 1993).

Work by two or more authors. For works by two authors, put the authors' names in a sentence or within the parentheses with the page number. Within parentheses (but not in a sentence), use "&" between the names: (Kadushin & Martin, 1981).

For works by three to five authors, name all of the authors in your first reference: (Vissing, Straus, Gelles & Harrop, 1991). In subsequent references, both in the text and within parentheses, use only the last name of the first author followed by *et al.* (meaning "and others"): (Vissing et al., 1991).

For works by six or more authors, use only the last name of the first author and *et al.* for even the first citation: (Baher et al., 1967).

Work by corporate (group) author. When the "author" of a source is a corporation or other organization, use the organization's full name in a sentence or within the parentheses: (National Center on Child Abuse and Neglect, 1992).

However, if the organization has a long name and a familiar abbreviation, you may use the abbreviation after the first citation. To do so, show the abbreviation in the first citation in brackets after the full name: (National Institutes of Health [NIH], 1995). Then in subsequent citations, use only the abbreviation: (NIH, 1995).

No author given. When the author's name is unknown, use the first few words of the title. If the title is of a book or periodical, underline it. If it is of an article, put it within quotation marks.

> The article "Spanking may foster aggression" (1995)
>
> states that parental anger when spanking is key.

> An article in <u>The Menninger Letter</u> states that parental
>
> anger when spanking is key ("Spanking may foster
>
> aggression," 1995).

(The full title of the article is "Spanking May Foster Aggression Toward Peers in Young Children." Note that in APA style, the only words capitalized in the title are the first word, the first word of any subtitle [a secondary title that follows a colon], and proper nouns.)

Personal communication. Conversations, letters, memos, E-mail and other personal unpublished communications should be cited within parentheses by name and date as follows: (M. Clark, personal communication, January 10, 1996). If the person's name is included in the sentence, then only the words *personal communication* and the date need to be within the parentheses. In the APA system, personal communications are cited only within the text, not in the list of references.

38b APA list of references

Begin the list of citations on a separate sheet of paper with the title *References* centered at the top. Number each page in Arabic numerals, consecutively from the last page of text of your paper, at least one inch from the paper's right edge, between the top of the paper and the first line of the text. Include the first two or three words of your paper's title above each page number or five spaces before it. Double-space throughout, including between the title and the first citation.

Give all authors' names for all entries; do not use *et al.* For all authors of a given work, list the last name first followed by the initials.

Put the date of publication in parentheses immediately after the author's name. If an author has written more than one work in the list, repeat the full name, and list the titles by the date of publication. If two or more titles by the same author have the same date of publication, assign a lower-case letter to each (*a, b,* and so on). Write the letter immediately after the date: (1993a).

Alphabetize the entries by the last name of the author or editor (or first author or editor). If no author or editor is given for a work or if two or more titles by the same author have the same date of publication, alphabetize according to the first word of the title other than *a, an,* or *the.*

For each entry, use a format called a **hanging indent**, in which every line in a paragraph except for the first one is indented. (For manuscripts intended for publication, each citation should begin with a paragraph indent, with subsequent lines flush with the left margin. This format will be typeset as a hanging indent.) Double-space throughout.

A sample "References" list is on page 68. Following are models of various types of citations for an APA-style list of references.

Books and other nonperiodicals. In general, there are four main parts to APA book citations:

1. The author's or editor's name (last name first, first and middle initials only).

2. The copyright date or, for an unpublished work, the year the work was produced (in parentheses).

3. The work's title and any subtitle (underlined). Capitalize only the first word in the title, the first word of a subtitle (a secondary title that follows a colon), and proper nouns.

4. Place of publication and publisher. If the place of publication is a city well known for publishing and will not be confused with another place, use only the city name. Otherwise add a U.S. Postal Service abbreviation of the state or the full name of the country. If several cities are listed, give the one where the home office is located, if indicated, or the first city listed. Use the full name of the publisher, but you may omit such terms as *Co., Inc.,* and *Publishers.* However, do not omit the words *Books* and *Press.*

This basic format is illustrated below with a book by one author, followed by examples of other types of book entries.

Book by one author

Gleick, J. (1993). Genius: The life and science of Richard Feynman. New York: Vintage Books.

Book by two or more authors

Peters, T., & Austin, N. (1985). A passion for excellence. New York: Random House.

Book with corporate (group) author

Rand McNally & Company. (1975). The magnificent continent. Chicago: Author.

(The word *author* indicates that the author is also the publisher.)

Book with no author or editor given

The inventive Yankee: From rockets to roller skates, 200 years of Yankee inventors and inventions. (1989). Dublin, NH: Yankee Books.

Anthology

Schilpp, P. A. (Ed.). (1959). Albert Einstein: Philosopher-scientist. New York: Harper.

Edition of an author's work prepared by an editor

Franklin, B. (1931). The ingenious Dr. Franklin: Selected scientific letters of Benjamin Franklin (N. G. Goodman, Ed.). Philadelphia: University of Pennsylvania Press.

Translation

Wallenberg, R. (1995). Letters and dispatches 1924-1944 (K. Board, Trans.). New York: Arcade.

Second or subsequent edition

Kaplan, H., Bally, J. B., & Garretson, C. (1987). Speechreading: A way to improve understanding (2nd ed.). Washington, DC: Gallaudet University Press.

Multivolume work

Gänzl, K. (1994). The encyclopedia of the musical theatre (Vol. 1). New York: Schirmer Books.

(If you are using more than one volume of a multivolume work, cite the volumes used: *Vols. 1-6.*)

Work in an anthology

Heller, J. (1982). TV news for teens. In M. Schwarz (Ed.), TV & teens (pp. 31-34). Reading, MA: Addison-Wesley.

(Note that for a work in an anthology, page numbers are given and that the abbreviations *p.* and *pp.* are used for *page* and *pages.*)

Article in a reference book

Smylie, J. H. (1994). Faith healing. In Encyclopedia Americana (Vol. 10, pp. 849-850). Danbury, CT: Grolier.

Brochure or pamphlet

Smithsonian Institution. (1985). After the revolution: Everyday life in America 1780-1800 [Brochure]. Washington, DC: Author.

Dissertation abstract

Stitt, M. (1993). Post-traumatic stress disorder and battered women (Doctoral dissertation, Fordham University, 1993). Dissertation Abstracts International, 54, 2225B.

(When the source is on microfilm or CD-ROM, the medium and the access number are included.)

Unpublished doctoral dissertation

Gonzalez, A. M. (1993). The Hispanic patient: Clinical issues, ethical concerns and implications for professional practice in mental health. Unpublished doctoral dissertation, Widener University, Chester, PA.

Periodicals. In general, there are four main parts to APA citations for articles in periodicals:

1. The author's name (last name first, first and middle initials only).

2. The date of publication (in parentheses). For magazines, newspapers, and newsletters, include the month. Spell out every month fully; do not abbreviate.

3. The title of the article (without quotation marks or underlining). Capitalize only the first word in the title, the first word of a subtitle, and proper nouns.

4. Publication information: the periodical title (underlined; capitalized according to the usual rules for capitalizing proper nouns), the volume number (underlined) of journals and magazines, and the pages. Put commas between the elements in this section. Use the abbreviations *p.* (for *page*) and *pp.* (for *pages*) only before the page numbers of articles in newspapers.

If there is no volume number, include the year followed by a comma, a space, and the month or season after the author's name.

Following are models of types of periodical citations in the APA style.

Article in a journal with continuous pagination from issue to issue in an annual volume

Weiss, T. G. (1995). The United Nations at fifty: Recent lessons. Current History, 94, 223-228.

(Use the full page numbers—for example, 223–228, *not* 223–28.)

Article in a journal with separate pagination for each issue

Klamer, K. (1995). Minority leader. Vocational Education Journal, 70 (5), 36-37, 46.

(The issue number is in parentheses.)

Article in a magazine

Weekly

Begley, S. (1995, March 27). Gray matters. Newsweek, 125, 48-54.

Monthly

Rock, M. (1995, March). Human 'moms' teach chimps it's all in the family. Smithsonian, 25, 70-75.

Article in a newspaper

Goleman, D. (1993, June 13). Provoking a patient's worst fears to determine the brain's role. The New York Times, pp. C1, C10.

Editorial

False promise. (1995, June 5). [Editorial.] Philadelphia Inquirer, p. A8.

(For a letter to the editor, replace *Editorial* with *Letter to the Editor*.)

Review

Jackson, D. D. (1994). [Review of the book The Story of Webster's Third]. Smithsonian, 25, 146-147.

Other sources. Following are models for citations for several other types of sources.

Videocassette

Guggenheim, C. (Producer). (1992). A time for justice: America's civil rights movement [Videocassette]. Montgomery, AL: Teaching Tolerance.

Sound recording

Taylor, J. (1991). Copperline. On New moon shine [CD]. New York: Columbia Records.

(Put within parentheses whatever format is appropriate, such as *CD, cassette,* or *LP*.)

On-line sources

Minsky, M. (1994). Will robots inherit the Earth? [4 pp.]. Scientific American [On-line serial], 271 (4). Available: America Online: Scientific American Online.

National Research Council Committee on Virtual Reality Research and Development. (1995). Technology gap exists between what is virtual and what is reality [On-line]. Available: America Online: NAS Online.

Koehn, D. (1995, July). The ethics of handwriting
analysis in pre-employment screening
[34 paragraphs]. The On-Line Journal of Ethics
[On-line serial], 1. Available: Internet:
http://condor.depaul.edu/ethics/hand.html

(The APA prefers that material available in both print and electronic forms be cited in print form. While the 1995 edition of the *Publication Manual of the American Psychological Association* provides some model citations of electronically accessed material, it states, "At the time of writing this edition, a standard had not yet emerged for referencing on-line information." The manual goes on to point out that citations of electronic sources, like others, should have two basic goals: credit to the author and sufficient information for the reader to find the cited material. In general, for APA-style citations for on-line sources, include the author, date, and title as you would for a print citation. In place of the publication information given for books, add an availability statement that includes the information necessary to access the material. [The APA's recommendations for on-line sources are based on the 1993 book *Electronic Style: A Guide to Citing Electronic Information*, by Li and Crane.])

Computer software

Anger [CD-ROM]. (1993). The new Grolier multimedia
encyclopedia. Danbury, CT: Grolier Electronic
Publishing.

(If the article is signed, begin with the author's name followed by the date, writing both in the usual APA style.)

Sample References List: APA Format

Corporal Punishment   14

References

Agnew, R. (1983). Physical punishment and delinquency.
Youth & Society, 15, 225-236.

Harris, J. R., & Liebert, R. (1987). The child: Development
through birth to adolescence (2d ed.). New York:
Prentice Hall.

Samalin, N. (1992, July). What's wrong with spanking? Parents
Magazine [On-line serial], 67. Available: CompuServe,
Magazine Database Plus, Reference #A16886244.

Spanking may foster aggression toward peers in young
children. (1995, March). The Menninger Letter, 3, 1-2.

Stark, E. (1989, December). Spare the rod in schools, but not at
home. Psychology Today, 3, 10.

Straus, M. A. (1994). Beating the devil out of them: Corporal
punishment in American families. New York: Macmillan.

Straus, M. A. (1992a). Children as witness to marital violence:
A risk factor for life-long problems among a nationally
representative sample of American men and women. In
D. F. Schwartz (Ed.), Children and violence: Report of
the twenty-third Ross roundtable on critical approaches
to common pediatric problems (pp. 98-109). Columbus,
OH: Ross Laboratories.

Straus, M. A. (1992b). Sociological research and social policy:
The case of family violence. Sociological Forum, 7,
211-237.